822·33
T I

THE BBC TV SHAKESPEARE
Literary Consultant: John Wilders

JULIUS CAESAR

ENTERED

THE BBC TV SHAKESPEARE

AS YOU LIKE IT
JULIUS CAESAR
MEASURE FOR MEASURE
RICHARD II
ROMEO AND JULIET

THE BBC TV SHAKESPEARE

Literary Consultant: John Wilders
Fellow of Worcester College, Oxford

Julius Caesar

BRITISH BROADCASTING CORPORATION

Published by the
British Broadcasting Corporation
35 Marylebone High Street
London W1M 4AA

ISBN 0 563 17616 4

This edition first published 1979
© The British Broadcasting Corporation
and the Contributors 1979

The text of the Works of Shakespeare
edited by Peter Alexander
© William Collins Sons and Company Ltd 1951

The text of *Julius Caesar* used in this volume is the Alexander
text, edited by the late Professor Peter Alexander and chosen by
the BBC as the basis for its television production, and is
reprinted by arrangement with William Collins Sons and
Company Ltd. The complete Alexander text is published in one
volume by William Collins Sons and Company Ltd under the
title *The Alexander Text of the Complete Works of William
Shakespeare*.

All photographs are BBC copyright (David Edwards)

Printed in England at
The Pitman Press, Bath

CONTENTS

PREFACE

Cedric Messina

The plays of William Shakespeare have been performed not only in theatres, but also in country houses, inns and courtyards, and one of the earliest references to performances was made by William Keeting, a Naval Commander who kept a journal of a voyage to the East Indies in 1607. The entry for 5 September, off the coast of Sierra Leone, refers to a performance of *Hamlet*, and that of 30 September to a performance of *Richard II*, both being staged for Portuguese visitors aboard the East India Company's ship *Dragon*. And so the plays started their triumphant progress of performances throughout the civilised world.

If sheer numbers of productions in London, Stratford-upon-Avon and America during the twentieth century are anything to go by, *Julius Caesar* must be the most performed of all Shakespeare's plays, not excepting *Romeo and Juliet*. It is included in the curriculum of almost every English and Drama course in the United Kingdom and the USA and generations of schoolchildren are inclined to take Shakespeare's play as the truth of history, believing that the ancient Romans spoke in iambic pentameters. Perhaps the masterstroke of 'Et tu Brute?' in Latin has something to do with making the dramatic seem historic.

Julius Caesar has been heard on the radio, seen in the theatre, presented on television, and filmed more than once. Perhaps the best-known reference to it is by Polonius in *Hamlet* when he says he has seen a play in which Caesar is murdered in the Capitol, although Shakespeare does not claim the authorship for himself. The three great roles of Brutus, Mark Antony and Cassius have been essayed by most of the great classical actors of the twentieth century. Although not a very large role, the part of Julius Caesar permeates the whole play, and after his death his spirit haunts the three other protagonists, two of whom, Brutus and Antony, he had numbered amongst his greatest friends in life. Loyalty, envy and treachery are the framework of the play. In this century *Julius Caesar* has had many productions on film and on stage in the

United States of America. John Gielgud played Cassius in the American film with Marlon Brando as a fascinating Mark Antony, and a modern-dress production directed by Orson Welles had a great success on Broadway in the 1930s. The Fascist implications of the production were widely commented upon at the time. In this production Keith Michell, known throughout the world as the television Henry VIII, plays Mark Antony. Brutus is played by one of the splendid actors of the Royal Shakespeare Company, Richard Pasco. He is an actor of great distinction in the UK, and has been seen on stage in America in a series of Poetry Recitals with HSH The Princess Grace of Monaco.

BBC Television is not inexperienced in the presentation of the plays of Shakespeare, and indeed as early as 1937, on the first regular television service in the world, it presented a full-length version of *Julius Caesar*. Since then thirty of the plays have been presented, the more popular ones many times over. Some have been produced in encapsulated form like *An Age of Kings*; some done on location like *Hamlet* at Elsinore with Christopher Plummer as the Prince and Robert Shaw as Claudius, and *Twelfth Night* at Castle Howard in Yorkshire with Janet Suzman leading the cast as Viola. Studio productions have included *The Tragedy of King Lear*, and *The Merchant of Venice* with Maggie Smith as a memorable Portia. Many productions have been taken from the theatre and translated into television terms like the Royal Shakespeare Company's *The Wars of the Roses* and The National Theatre Zeffirelli production of *Much Ado About Nothing*.

In the discharging of its many duties as a Public Broadcasting Service the BBC has presented during the last ten years, at peak viewing time on BBC I on every fourth Sunday night, *Play of the Month*, a series of classical productions ranging from all the major plays of Chekhov to a number of Shavian masterpieces. Aeschylus has been produced in the series, and so have many of the plays of William Shakespeare. So not only in the presentation of Shakespeare, but also in the translation to the screen of the great dramatic statements of all ages and countries, has the BBC demonstrated that it is fully equipped to meet the enormous challenge of *The BBC Television Shakespeare*.

The autumn of 1975 gave birth to the idea of recording the complete canon of the thirty-seven plays of the national playwright. (Thirty-six of the plays were published in the First Folio of 1623, exactly half of which had never been published before. The thirty-seventh is *Pericles, Prince of Tyre*, first published in the

Quarto of 1609.) The first memo on the subject of televising all the plays emanated from my office on 3 November 1975, and was addressed to Alasdair Milne, then Director of Programmes, and now Managing Director, Television. We were asking for his blessing on the project. His reply was immediate and enthusiastic, as was that of the present Director-General, Ian Trethowan. This warm response to the idea stimulated us in the Plays Department to explore the possibility of making the plan a reality – six plays per year for six years, with one odd man out. It has been called the greatest project the BBC has ever undertaken.

There followed a succession of meetings, conferences, discussions and logistical quotations from engineers, designers, costume designers, make-up artists, financial advisers, educational authorities, university dons and musicians. The Literary Consultant, Dr John Wilders, was appointed, as was David Lloyd-Jones as Music Adviser. Alan Shallcross was made responsible for the preparation of the texts. On the island of Ischia, off the coast of Italy, Sir William Walton composed the opening fanfare for the title music for the series. Visits were made to the United States of America to finalise coproduction deals; decisions were taken about the length of the presentations, to average about two and a half hours per play, and more seriously, the order of their transmission. This was a game played by many interested parties, some suggesting the plays be presented chronologically, which would have meant the series opening with the comparatively unknown *Henry VI Parts 1, 2 and 3*. This idea was hastily abandoned. A judicious mixture of comedy, tragedy and history seemed the best answer to the problem. It was decided that the English histories, from *Richard II* through all the *Henry IVs, V* and *VIs* to *Richard III* would be presented in chronological order, so that some day in the not too distant future, the eight plays that form this sequence will be able to be seen in their historical order, a unique record of the chronicled history of that time. The plays that form the first sequence will be *Romeo and Juliet, Richard II, As You Like It, Julius Caesar, Measure for Measure* and *Henry VIII*.

The guiding principle behind *The BBC Television Shakespeare* is to make the plays, in permanent form, accessible to audiences throughout the world, and to bring to these many millions the sheer delight and excitement of seeing them in performances – in many cases for the first time. For students, these productions will offer a wonderful opportunity to study the plays performed by some of the greatest classical actors of our time. But it is a primary

8

intention that the plays are offered as entertainment, to be made as vividly alive as it is possible for the production teams to make them. They are not intended to be museum-like examples of past productions. It is this new commitment, for six plays of Shakespeare per year for six years, that makes the project unique.

In the thirty-seven plays there are a thousand speaking parts, and they demand the most experienced of actors and the most excellent of directors to bring them to life. In the field of directors we are very fortunate, for many of the brilliant practitioners in this series of plays have had wide experience in the classics, both on television and in the theatre. The directors are responsible for the interpretations we shall see, but as the series progresses it will be fascinating to see how many of the actors take these magnificent parts and make them their own.

It was decided to publish the plays, using the Peter Alexander edition, the same text as used in the production of the plays, and one very widely used in the academic world. But these texts with their theatrical divisions into scenes and acts are supplemented with their television equivalents. In other words we are also publishing the television scripts on which the production was based. There are colour and black and white photographs of the production, a general introduction to the play by Dr John Wilders, and an article by Henry Fenwick which includes interviews with the actors, directors, designers and costume designers, giving their reactions to the special problems their contributions encountered in the transfer of the plays to the screen. The volumes include a newly-compiled glossary and a complete cast list of the performers, including the names of the technicians, costume designers and scenic designers responsible for the play.

The First Folio includes in its thirty-seven plays the only authoritative text of *Julius Caesar*. Its comparative shortness combined with its excellence as a text suggests the play, in all probability, was set up for the Folio from an acting script used by Shakespeare's Company. No Quarto edition of the play was published until the latter half of the seventeenth century. The play has 2477 lines, of which thirteen have been cut; all the anachronisms, such as the striking clock, are retained, as shown in the accompanying text of the television production. *Julius Caesar* is eighteenth in the accepted chronological order of the plays, and this production was recorded on videotape at the BBC Television Centre, White City, London, in July 1978.

INTRODUCTION TO
JULIUS CAESAR

John Wilders

Julius Caesar is, among other things, a brilliantly constructed political thriller, an account of the origins, execution and consequences of a plot to assassinate the most powerful man in the western world. Throughout the first three acts Shakespeare creates a taut, steady suspense unequalled in any work he had written previously and surpassed only in the central acts of *Othello* which he composed about five years later. The gradual, subtle process whereby Iago persuades Othello of his wife's infidelity is, indeed, a development and refinement of the process whereby Cassius persuades Brutus of Caesar's dictatorial ambitions.

Shakespeare portrays the history of Rome, as he portrays the history of England, on the assumption that its victories and failures, its wars and revolutions are determined by the personalities – or rather the relationship between the personalities – of the few men who are in a position to control it, 'the choice and master spirits of this age', as Antony calls them. The play implies that Caesar was murdered and that Antony ultimately got the better of the conspirators only because Brutus and Cassius, Caesar and Antony were the kind of men they were. Had any one of their temperaments been different, Caesar would have remained alive and Roman history would have taken a different course. Hence the impassioned conversations between them carry, for them and for the audience, an unusual weight. We are made to realise that the fate of Rome depends on their influence on one another. There are other ways of accounting for historical change – as the effect of God's providential guidance, for example, or as the effect of social and economic conditions – but Shakespeare's way is very suitable for presentation as drama.

The conspiracy is portrayed as a delicate, complex human machine which will carry out its task only if every moving part in it, each character, performs its required function, and until the instant when the assassins' swords enter Caesar's body we sense that the machine may very easily break down. Even though we know as a historical fact that Caesar will be murdered, nevertheless the characters and the succession of events are so convincingly depicted that we have the sensation, no matter how often we may see the play performed, that this time, in this performance, the plot may fail: Brutus may not accede to the persuasions of Cassius, Caesar may decide not to go to the Capitol this morning or may, for once, choose to pay attention to Artemidorus' warning letter. The suspense arises from Shakespeare's portrayal of all the major scenes as processes of persuasion and choice, for, unlike the parts of an ordinary machine, human beings are apparently free agents who may make decisions of their own. Yet, at any rate in this play, they are not as free as they assume: their choices are determined by the nature of their personalities and their susceptibility to the persuasions of others.

The originator and motive force behind the conspiracy is Cassius, whose hostility towards Caesar arises from two motives, both of which he reveals when he attempts to enlist the support of Brutus. Cassius despises Caesar personally because he regards him as a man inferior to himself who possesses no natural right to command the lives of others:

> 'Brutus' and 'Caesar'. What should be in that 'Caesar'?
> Why should that name be sounded more than yours?
> Write them together: yours is as fair a name.
> Sound them: it doth become the mouth as well.
> Weigh them: it is as heavy. Conjure with 'em:
> 'Brutus' will start a spirit as soon as 'Caesar'.
> Now, in the name of all the gods at once,
> Upon what meat doth this our Caesar feed,
> That he is grown so great?

At the same time Cassius has – or at least claims to have – powerful republican convictions and believes that to submit to the authority of a king is beneath the dignity of a Roman citizen:

> Age, thou art sham'd!
> Rome, thou has lost the breed of noble bloods!
> When went there by an age, since the great flood,
> But it was fam'd with more than with one man?

Whether Cassius is genuinely motivated by political principles or not it is impossible to know. His republicanism may be as passionately felt as he says it is, but this honourable ideal, as he well knows, is precisely the principle to which Brutus will respond sympathetically, and he needs the support of Brutus.

Whereas in Cassius envy and public interest are apparently united in driving him towards the assassination (and it is this combination of motives which gives him his fierce energy), Brutus is, throughout the period before the murder, in a state of agonised indecision. On the one hand he prides himself on a high political rectitude which will not tolerate the possibility of a dictatorship; on the other hand he is a naturally fastidious man to whom murder is distasteful, especially the murder of Caesar who is his intimate friend. Until the scene (II i) when he makes a formal alliance with the conspirators he is in an intolerable dilemma, compelled to make a choice between two equally unacceptable alternatives. He can either refrain from allying himself with Cassius and thereby betray his principles, or join the faction and thereby betray his friendship with Caesar. No third course is available to him and he is allowed no opportunity to remain neutral. Even when he has committed himself to the latter course he still tries to find some way whereby he may destroy Caesar the institution without killing Caesar the man and thereby remain true to both his principles:

> O that we then could come by Caesar's spirit,
> And not dismember Caesar! But, alas,
> Caesar must bleed for it!

Recognising that the institution is inseparable from the man, Brutus then tries to make the murder palatable to himself by emphasising the motive and the manner in which the deed should be done:

> Let's kill him boldly, but not wrathfully,
> Let's carve him as a dish fit for the gods,
> Not hew him as a carcase fit for hounds.

He is able to co-operate in the plot only because he believes himself to be doing so for the highest political motives: he sees himself as a sacrificer not a butcher. By a terrible irony, however, Caesar, as he watches Brutus advance on him with his sword, totally misunderstands Brutus' motive. In the last moment of his life, with the words 'Et tu, Brute?', he accuses Brutus of betraying a personal trust.

The tension created in these first two acts is increased by a sustained dramatic irony at the expense of Caesar. Although he makes two impressive but brief appearances on his way to and from the games, all our attention is directed on the manoeuvres of his opponents. The crucially significant ceremony in which he is offered a crown takes place off stage and our interest is placed not on the incident itself but on the effect it has in strengthening the determination of the plotters. By the time they come to escort their victim to his death (II ii), Caesar is practically the only man in the theatre who is unaware of the imminent attempt which will be made on his life. The success of the enterprise depends, however, on the co-operation not only of the conspirators but of their victim: Caesar must be induced to come to the Capitol in order to receive the weapons his murderers have prepared for him. Here, again, Shakespeare prolongs and tightens the suspense by introducing another scene of persuasion and choice. Throughout the night before the murder there have been violent storms, unnatural portents have appeared in the sky, and Caesar's wife has had a dream that his statue is running with blood. Calphurnia's dream can be interpreted either as an omen of disaster, which is her own belief, or as a portent of good fortune, which is the interpretation offered by Decius Brutus. Caesar is compelled to choose between the former, in which case he will stay safely at home, and the latter, in which case he will go to the Capitol. He decides to believe Decius Brutus and, as a consequence, appears to the audience to submit voluntarily to his own assassination. He does so, it should be noted, not on the strength of the evidence, which allows either interpretation, but because Decius Brutus' version is flattering and Caesar is known to be as susceptible to flattery as Brutus is to the cause of honour.

Further suspense is added to these scenes by our knowledge that the plot is several times in danger of being exposed. Having been assaulted by the persuasions of Cassius, Brutus then has to receive the earnest and loving pleas of his wife that he should confess the reasons for his obvious disquiet. Once again, Brutus has to make a choice, this time between the intimate claims of marriage and those of his political allegiance. The domestic interview between them (at the end of II i) is therefore at the same time tender and full of risk. Even in the final seconds before the murder there is a risk that it will fail, for Caesar is handed a document in which all the details of the conspiracy are exposed, but which he chooses not to read. It is, then, with relief on behalf of the conspirators as well as terror on behalf of Caesar that we witness at last the deed towards which the play has so far been leading.

13

Shakespeare now uses his dramatic skill to revive our attention in the immediate aftermath of the murder, the point at which he is most likely to lose it. Political success in this play depends on a man's ability to foresee the future and thereby to prepare for it and, if possible, exploit the opportunities it offers. In this art Cassius is obviously more skilled than Brutus: he can predict that Brutus will respond to the call of duty and therefore enlists his support by appealing to that motive. Similarly Decius Brutus predicts that Caesar will be influenced by flattery and lures his victim into the open by flattering him. Yet none of the conspirators appears to have looked beyond the assassination to its possible consequences. They assume that by destroying a potential tyrant they have initiated a new era of 'peace, freedom and liberty' and begin to leave the Capitol as though their task was finished. They are met, however, by a messenger who unwittingly holds the power by which the murder will have results quite different from those they expect. For the messenger comes from Mark Antony who, by his skill in manipulating the emotions of the mob, will turn public opinion powerfully against the conspirators and thereby set off a civil war. The entry of the messenger is the first sign of the movement of the play, and of history, into a new phase, and his speech is a transposition into it. Yet, with the arrival of a second messenger Shakespeare hints that Antony's period of supremacy will itself be overtaken by a period in which he is controlled by the as yet unseen figure of Octavius. *Julius Caesar* shows the rise and fall of successive individuals – Pompey (whose former popularity and subsequent assassination is referred to in the opening scene), Caesar, Brutus, Cassius and Antony – in the larger context of Roman history.

Shakespeare's theatrical sense shows itself as much in his talent for concealment as in his subtlety of revelation. We see far less of Octavius Caesar, for example, than of any other significant character in this play: his first, subdued appearance comes not until the fourth act. Yet this unknown youth will eventually be the last survivor from the play and will, after it is over, become the Emperor Augustus, a leader of far greater power than Caesar. Similarly Mark Antony, whose presence dominates the middle of the action, appears very briefly at the beginning and is usually mentioned slightingly as a lightweight, a playgoer who 'revels long o'nights'. By the middle of the third act he has become transformed into a subtle and commanding orator who, for a while, is in sole charge of the political situation. His character acquires a sudden depth and seriousness of purpose. It seems that the sight of Caesar's body and the realisation that this giant has been reduced to non-existence create emotions in him which either we have not been allowed to glimpse or of which he has not hitherto been capable:

O mighty Caesar! dost thou lie so low?
Are all thy conquests, glories, triumphs, spoils,
Shrunk to this little measure? Fare thee well.

When he first confronts and is encircled by the conspirators, however, he can save himself only by his wits.

Brutus, with characteristically simple trust, is content to allow Antony's request to deliver the funeral oration over Caesar's body; Cassius, sharper and more sceptical, instinctively foresees the dangerous purposes for which Antony may use his oration. Antony's fate (and Rome's) rests on a brief struggle of wills between Brutus and Cassius (III ii 232–44) in which Brutus, with catastrophic results, prevails. Meanwhile the audience waits to see which of their predictions will prove correct.

Each of the funeral orations – Brutus' and Antony's – reflects the character of the speaker. Brutus' speech, in prose, is sober, lucid and has the balanced sentence structure typical of a logical, thoughtful scholar:

If then that friend demand why Brutus rose against Caesar, this is my answer: Not that I lov'd Caesar less, but that I lov'd Rome more. Had you rather Caesar were living and die all slaves, than that Caesar were dead, to live all free men? As Caesar lov'd me, I weep for him; as he was fortunate, I rejoice at it; as he was valiant, I honour him; but – as he was ambitious, I slew him.

He innocently assumes that the masses are as rational as himself. Antony's oration, in verse, whips up the emotions of the mob to a state of hysteria without their realising that they are being manipulated. Throughout, Antony claims not to be using the methods he actually practises: he claims not to praise Caesar but then proceeds to do so; he claims to applaud Brutus for his honourable nature while actually casting doubt on it; he claims not to disprove Brutus' argument yet repeatedly refutes it; he claims to be fearful of rebellion while actually inciting it; he refuses to read Caesar's will, but reveals its contents, ostensibly at the request of the people but in fact to suit his own purposes; he seems to be overcome with grief but displays it calculatedly. Hence, when the crowd are roused to mutiny, they believe they have made the decision for themselves. In a play full of scenes of persuasion and crises of choice, this is the most prolonged and powerful. The people have a choice between believing Brutus' account of Caesar as a tyrant and Antony's portrayal of him as generous and compassionate. They choose the latter version not because it is necessarily more reliable but because it is more movingly conveyed. By the time Antony's speech is finished, Brutus and Cassius have fled from Rome in panic.

Shortly after his public appearance, we are shown the supposedly impulsive Antony in private, determining with Octavius which of their potential enemies shall be eliminated. The man who wept on the death of Caesar now casually agrees to the murder of his own nephew. With this scene, the first extended, unified and consistently tense movement of the play concludes and the action is transferred to the battlefield for the civil war which Antony's oratory and Brutus' misplaced trust have provoked.

Julius Caesar never regains the momentum and consistency of suspense which have so far been its most impressive achievements. This is partly because the last two acts are episodic, partly because there is insufficient playing time left for Shakespeare to give to the deaths of Cassius and Brutus the dramatic weight and length of attention they deserve. The last section of the play does, however, contain one great scene, again a clash of temperaments. During most of the so-called 'quarrel scene' (IV iii) between Brutus and Cassius, Shakespeare does little to advance the plot, but he does expose, with wonderful psychological insight, the opposition between their two temperaments which has been apparent since their first appearance but is now brought into the open. Cassius, as always, is full of nervous energy, spontaneous, yet wary and practical; Brutus maintains his moral idealism even when it requires that he should accuse and reprimand his friend. Both realise that, in their bickering, they are violating their friendship and the principles which formerly united them, so that their outbursts of temper are interspersed with waves of remorse and embarrassment. Throughout the scene Shakespeare controls the emotional temperature in such a way as to sustain the attention of the audience while remaining faithful to the temperaments of the two characters. It is only towards the end of their encounter that Brutus confesses why he has been uncharacteristically irritable: his wife has committed suicide. This revelation gives him the moral advantage over Cassius so that the latter accedes with little protest to Brutus' plan of attack for the forthcoming battle. For purely temperamental reasons, the more astute, hard-headed Cassius gives way to the judgement of Brutus and the prophetic words of Caesar's ghost warn us that, as always, Brutus has made an error of judgement. He has 'misconstrued everything'.

Shakespeare's view of this crucial period of history is, throughout, ironical, in the sense that he, and through him the audience, has a better grasp of politics and war than the characters engaged in them. This effect is made possible because, unlike the protagonists who peer uncertainly into the future, guessing what may happen and usually acting on false conjectures, we ourselves know what the outcome will be. The play illustrates how, in Cicero's words,

Men may construe things after their fashion,
Clean from the purpose of the things themselves.

But Shakespeare's ironies are also of other kinds: the fate of Rome depends not on the will of the people but on the contests between the few to influence them; the fastidious Brutus finds himself reluctantly drawn into an alliance with a 'faction' whom he despises; the conspirators, in their attempt to establish peace, provoke a war; the most morally upright character, Brutus, is the most politically inept, whereas the most astute, Cassius, gives way to Brutus in those decisions which are most fatal, and Brutus is destroyed by the very qualities which, in a different context, would be admirable: his honesty and trust. For all their courage, self-confidence and strength of will, these men are shown to be pitifully limited in their freedom of choice and their understanding of the public world of which they believe themselves masters.

Julius Caesar was probably written in 1599, shortly after the English history plays, *Henry IV Parts 1 and 2* and *Henry V*, which it resembles in its preoccupation with politics, civil war and the relationship and tensions between personal loyalties and public duty. The language and style of *Julius Caesar* is not nearly so varied nor the range of characters so wide as those of the English histories, and there is very little comedy in it. This is probably because Shakespeare was trying to convey the impression of a Roman rather than an English way of life. Having been educated as a schoolboy in the Latin language and literature and in Roman history, he was well prepared to depict its civilisation. *Julius Caesar* resembles another of his Roman plays, *Coriolanus*, written about eight years later, in its grasp of the Roman sense of honour, an ideal which corresponds to patriotism and public duty, its portrayal of the dangerous power and instability of the plebeians, its sympathy for stoical self-control (shown particularly in Brutus and in his noble concept of suicide), and its emphasis on public orations which actually played an important part in Roman life.

THE PRODUCTION

Henry Fenwick

It would be hard to say whether 'Romeo, Romeo, wherefore art thou Romeo', 'To be or not to be, that is the question', or 'Friends, Romans, countrymen, lend me your ears' is the most quoted line in Shakespeare. Certainly *The Tragedy of Julius Caesar* ranks high in popular appeal. 'In people's minds it's history,' says Cedric Messina. 'The events of the play are thought of as literal historical incidents. Everybody thinks that Caesar really said "Et tu, Brute" when he was dying, they believe that lions roared in the Capitol before Caesar's death, that Antony actually said "Friends, Romans, countrymen, lend me your ears". People accept the details of the play as historical accounts. Youngsters read the play at school and it stays in their minds. It was popular among the Elizabethans too. It's one of the simpler plays and the Elizabethans regarded it as a picture of a great empire, which they themselves were also building up. They identified the greatness of Rome and the greatness of Elizabethan England. Some people think the Elizabethans knew more about Rome than modern people do: I doubt that, but they probably all read Caesar in Latin anyway and they certainly were interested in Rome.'

'It is a very tightly written play,' says director Herbert Wise. 'The plot moves at an enormous pace. It is certainly very popular with young people: one of the reasons, I think, is that it contains fewer contemporary jokes, fewer contemporary references, than many of Shakespeare's other plays. Like the other histories, *Julius Caesar* relies on its action, on its plot. And there is no sub-plot; the narrative line is very direct. It's: here's Caesar, is he going to get killed? Yes – he's killed. Are the conspirators going to get away with it? It must be Shakespeare's most direct play.'

For BBC audiences Herbert Wise is probably most easily identified as the director of the immensely successful *I, Claudius*, and I ask producer Cedric Messina whether Wise's triumph with his portrayal of Imperial Rome had anything to do with his selection as director for this play about the end of Republican

Rome. 'If anybody knows a toga, he does,' says Messina lightly. 'He's a director of great power and great original ability. His bringing to life of the family of Augustus Caesar – who incidentally makes a fleeting appearance here – was quite remarkable. But he's a director who's done an enormous amount of classical work of all sorts and it shows.'

The experience of *I, Claudius* was of little help or relevance in working on *Julius Caesar*, Wise says. '*Julius Caesar* is not really a Roman play. It's an Elizabethan play and it's a view of Rome from an Elizabethan standpoint. Apart from the anachronisms – and there are many of those: Brutus, in the conspiracy scene, says "Count the clock" and it strikes three when mechanical clocks weren't invented until about the twelfth or thirteenth centuries; a book has its leaf turned down when in Rome books didn't exist, there were slates or scrolls; there's a reference to the expressions on actors' faces and in Rome actors always wore masks – but anachronisms apart, the very essences of the play are really Tudor, not Roman. Shakespeare has caught the Roman flavour in the public speeches but I didn't feel that this was really a Roman play at all. Not that *Claudius* was necessarily a Roman play but at least it took a twentieth-century look, a very modern look, at Rome. This was quite different. There were not even the factual details of the background in common because Shakespeare made so many mistakes; he didn't really care whether he got it right or not. There are all sorts of contemporary references and details: there are references to wearing hoods over the head, to plucking people by the sleeves, but Romans almost never wore cloaks, certainly not hooded ones, and they didn't have any sleeves. The play was originally written to be done in contemporary dress with a toga thrown over the top – hence the references to sleeves, or to doublets being unbound. You can't unbind a doublet in Roman dress.'

Has there been any temptation to dress the play the way the Elizabethans dressed it, rather than in strict Roman style, I asked. 'I don't think that's right for the audience we will be getting,' says Wise. 'It's not a jaded theatre audience seeing the play for the umpteenth time: for them that would be an interesting approach and might throw new lights on the play. But for an audience many of whom won't have seen the play before, I believe it would only be confusing.' In fact, the play is being dressed with scrupulous accuracy in the fashions of Caesar's Rome. But that is not so simple as it sounds, and Odette Barrow does not appreciate the suggestion that all she has to do is clean the togas left over from *I, Claudius*. The clothes of Imperial Rome, she points out with polite scorn, were much too decorated and decadent to be used for the earlier period of *Julius Caesar*. Not only that, but it turns out that *Julius Caesar* has not been properly dressed in previous stage productions, so there is not much that is suitable for her to hire even for the battle scenes. Time has been tight: for the Shakespeare plays she has had approximately two months apiece to research, design and have the clothes made up. That is always pressured. Even with the resources of the BBC costume department some stuff must be hired. "You phone around various costumers and contacts to see if they actually have anything, then you have to go in person and sort it out yourself to see exactly what they have. What you're asking for they may *think* they have but when you get there you find out they haven't got it or it isn't right. It is pretty difficult. And so much of Shakespeare now is produced in a contemporary manner that the clothes from other productions are absolutely useless for what I need.'

To add to the normally tight schedule her research turned up recent information about Roman clothing and armour which showed that the designs many previous productions have used were actually incorrect. Work by Russell Robinson and Peter Connolly shows armour that is appreciably different from what is readily available. The discovery threw her into something of a spin: when we met, just before the play went into the studio, she had workers hurriedly knitting chain mail, modifying helmets and breast plates which weren't quite right, and she awaited news from Rome of a possible supply of correct helmets – which probably wouldn't arrive in time, anyway.

While showing me the accurate designs for Roman armour of the period she also turns up, on a page of *The Clothing of the Ancient Romans*, a sample of enormously varied colours, ranging from a pale pinky grey to a rather blue-tinged crimson. That, she tells me, is the range that the Romans referred to as purple. 'They didn't have our royal purple – their purple depended on their dyes and varied with them. They weren't in fact true purples as we know them – they ranged from reddy winey shades to slightly bluey reds. But on the television monitor you have to be careful what you choose. Obviously you want a colour that modern audiences will recognise as purple and you want one that's not going to come out too light or too dark. This one, you see, is too blue – that one's too red, it would come out almost black on the monitor. Quite often it depends what studio you're in as to what colours you can get away with. In some studios there's an overpowering magenta colour so you have to be careful about what you use; I think it's the cameras that do it: some have a slightly greeny tinge, though it's much better nowadays than it was. If you know what studio you're going into it will influence your way of using reds.' She shows me proudly the mulberry shade she has finally selected as being true to the actual Roman range of vegetable dyes, and as being able to come over on television as a recognisable purple.

She confesses, since I'm obviously sufficiently awed by the design problems I knew nothing about, that she will in fact be able to use some of the togas and tunics from *I, Claudius* – properly modified. 'I'm taking some of the decorations off the *I, Claudius* tunics and some of the togas can be used – though the imperial togas were very much larger. In this period they're much smaller and everything is very much simpler and stricter. Even the armour is much plainer than is usually used. Quite often, I think, Hollywood puts the full works on, with soldiers in the sort of elaborate armour they would only have used for triumphs and for festivals. They would have used a much plainer armour for fighting. For Mark Antony, because he's a general, I'll give him some ornamentation. The officers wore an almost Greek type of armour; the legionaries wore just a tunic and over that chain mail, with sandals, leather belt, sword and very plain helmet. And the lesser people really had very little protection at all.'

It may sound heretical, Herbert Wise confesses, but 'I don't think Shakespeare is ideally suited to television, and in my view no one in the past has really cracked it. I have several ideas about it and I hope that in this play I have taken some steps towards reconciling the Shakespearian experience in the theatre to television. I think that *Julius Caesar* is one of the few of his plays that are more suited to television because it is a bit of a thriller and the movement inside the play is continuous. The central static passages are few and far between and the plot is carried along all the time.

'One of the things I have tried very hard to do in this production is to be as *clear* as possible throughout the play,' Wise stresses. 'We have constantly asked ourselves: "What are we saying?" Not only *why* are we saying it, but what exactly are we saying, what are we talking about, so that the meaning should become clear. I think we have achieved that. Many of the comments of the crew working on it have been how clear it was, how easy to understand. Also the style in which I've done it – which can only be described as stylised naturalism – I only hope that in the way I've done it we've also done something towards clarifying the whole play. At least in the early part of the play, before we get to the battles, I haven't treated it in a naturalistic way – by which I mean, if we are supposed to be in a street, we are in a street, but there are no passers-by, there's nobody going in and out because it just clutters up the issue. Instead we concentrate on the main characters. We haven't stylised in such a way that there's a signpost up labelled "Street": that's always worrying for television. There's no question or doubt that you're in a street but there's nobody about, there're no shops, there's nothing happening that you would expect to happen in a street, so all the focus is on the main characters.

'When we get to the battle scenes at the end I have become more naturalistic. I thought, when we began doing them, "Well, we can't just have a couple of fellows ritually fighting, it would look ludicrous. You'll have to set up a real fight." And then the moment you have a real fight you have to set up a lot of real grass and before you know it you're in a naturalistic setting. Perhaps I could have stylised more – but you can only try it out.'

The battle scenes of Shakespeare seem to make all the directors uneasy, though Wise is the only one so far to have tackled the problem head on. If he is uncertain of his solution, his self-doubts don't seem to be shared by anyone else on the production. In the studio, as Wise anxiously supervised the appearance of the battlefield and delicately added ground mist to shroud the studio floor and wreathe the horses' feet, others shook their heads indulgently. It looked marvellous, they assured him, marvellous. But Wise seems to be a man who can't be assured by others.

Tony Abbott, the set designer, had obviously delighted in working with him. In his office, when I visited him, he was surrounded by photographs of things Roman. On his drawing board stands a model studio floor scattered with scale representations of bits of wall, rows of pillars, steps, columns and statues. In a few moves, like a grandmaster at chess, he was able to transform the model of Caesar's house into a Roman street, the steps of the forum, the Senate. The principle behind the construction is the same as that he used in his *Richard II* sets: each arrangement of scenery is made up of small units of architecture, capable of being realigned, reversed or added to. 'The units are all double-sided, so by turning them to show their other side you can change their scale. One column is much like another but put props against the basic architecture and you can change the environment completely. Move an archway to the end of a row of pillars and you open up a whole new perspective; add steps and a statue and you have created a totally new appearance.

'To create the basic units you have to abstract the essential elements of the architecture. I had a pile of research material that high,' he gestures, dismissing the numerous pictures and photos he has already shown me. 'What is essential is the grandeur, the scale of Rome. That's difficult in television, when everything looks smaller than it is. Lighting is integral to the effect; it's a crucial part of creating the environment and the image. Without the right lighting the best set can't work, but the lighting can actually create an atmosphere for the set to work in.

'Most productions you have to overdress, slightly. Shakespeare is in a sense more clear-cut and with Herbie there was the opportunity to exercise a certain simplicity. We didn't want to make the scenes too realistic: filling up the picture with details would be a distraction. We swept all that away. A lot of Shakespeare is self-explanatory and you don't need a lot of clutter. We wanted something crisper, something clear, something a lot of people can understand. The action relies on dialogue rather than a lot of movement, and instead of having props all over the place, as you have in the majority of television productions, we went for the simple answer. We had streets that were bare except for a few leaves blowing about: if you leave it crisp and simple you make your statement and get a more dramatic effect.'

'The play is obviously written for a theatre without scenery,' Wise points out, 'and the words are everything. The one thing television is is a visual medium, so if you introduce the visual things you don't need the words. The words and the visual elements are fighting each other all the time, and to find the right balance between the two things, where each shot actually tells and furthers the story and its relationship to what's being said inside the shot – these are the sort of things I found difficult and which you don't get in a modern play. In a modern play there are long passages where there is no dialogue at all, just a series of pictures or events. And because these plays are being done at least partly for educational purposes the brief is to cut or to alter as little as possible and to stick to the accepted, original text. So you can't take liberties the way you can with a modern play. We have left out the odd line, the odd word, but that's the exception rather than the rule. I've left the anachronisms in because I got to like them, I found them rather charming. The lines we've cut are ones like "Here comes Antony" when quite plainly here he comes. Brutus, in his orchard in the middle of the night, finds a letter and says:

> The exhalations, whizzing in the air,
> Give so much light that I may read by them.

You don't need that kind of line on television, you can see that it's light, so we cut that. I think we cut perhaps a little more than ten lines – that's all.

'But the main task was to soften the rhetoric and make it more immediate. The soliloquies are both voice over and spoken – some lines are said, some are thought, there's nothing new about that. But I have tried something else – when the lines are only thought I have tried to get the effect that they are thought much faster than you could speak them. That sounds like a contradiction in terms, since somebody has to speak them, even in voice over, but what I mean is that they come much faster than you could actually declaim them on stage because thoughts come much faster and seem very much more immediate inside the head. I think that works very well. There's a long passage in the early third of the play when Brutus is in the orchard and he has a long – about three or four minutes – soliloquy of self-analysis and doubt and discussion with himself as to whether he should or shouldn't join in the conspiracy to kill Caesar. It works, I think, extremely well. And in general it affects the style of acting – to do it like that it can't be declamatory.'

Julius Caesar, though it has an enormous cast, is essentially a four-hander. It is hard to say that there is one clear-cut leading character. In spite of the title, Caesar himself is a comparatively small part in terms of time spent on stage (or screen). 'Why they call it *The Tragedy of Julius Caesar*,' Messina explains, 'is because his influence goes on and on after his death. He is killed in Act 3, Scene 1, but his presence dominates the later quarrel between Brutus and Cassius and goes on right till the end. When Cassius falls on his slave's sword he cries: "Caesar, thou art reveng'd." Brutus, when he finds Cassius' body, says: "O Julius Caesar, thou art mighty yet!" Even just before Brutus dies, in his very last speech, after he has stuck in the sword, he says: "Caesar, now be still." So though the part is not the biggest it's an overwhelming presence.'

For the rest, the play is divided between the two conspirators,

Cassius and Brutus, and Caesar's friend and avenger Mark Antony. Keith Michell has played Antony before on television, when the BBC performed the Roman plays, so he has played the part across the whole age range. He has also played the old Antony of *Antony and Cleopatra* on stage, so his experience of the part is deep. 'I suppose I must know something about the character,' he says. He sees him as a 'man of instinct', incapable of plotting a murder. 'He's a man of such warmth and truth I think he's incapable of deception of any kind. That, I think, is why the oration speech is probably difficult for him. He knows that the only way he can beat these men, who have cold-bloodedly assassinated Caesar, is to beat them at their own game. I think what happens is that he is going to do his best to win the mob over, and he gets carried away, his emotion gets the better of him and he really does win the crowd over. He's not an orator, he's just a very, very good leader of men. As an actor, you've got to find your way into the famous speeches so they don't become famous speeches. You don't just stand and start off with "Friends, Romans, Countrymen". You've got to have your crowd, you've got to fight them and win them and I think, as always in those crowd speeches, you have two characters: you have the speaker and you have the crowd, and that crowd is a vital element in the speech.'

David Collings plays Cassius, a complex part which in some ways seems a sketch for Iago in *Othello*, though Cassius is not so much a total villain as a corrupt and ambitious politician. 'There is a touch of Iago there but Cassius is a patrician,' Collings points out. He did a lot of background reading for the part, mainly in Plutarch's *Lives*, which he found of invaluable help in grasping the character. 'The part was a long time coming: after the murder he becomes a much more likeable character, much more human in adversity. He's a very practical man and all his decisions are correct, but unfortunately he's in awe of Brutus and Brutus makes a lot of mistakes. It's because of Brutus' mistakes that the conspirators finally fail.'

If anyone is the hero of the play it is the mistaken Brutus. 'Although he performs an extremely bloody deed and creates nothing but unhappiness he does it for honest reasons,' says Richard Pasco. 'For the good of the state and of his country. This is a man who was a *gentle* man; as Antony says: "His life was gentle." A man like that doesn't go round plunging daggers into people. The moment when everybody else has stabbed Caesar and Brutus comes up and gives the final blow – it was pretty difficult to steel myself to do that.'

'I believe *Julius Caesar* is the tragedy of Brutus,' says Wise, 'and I find Brutus immensely human. He does a terrible thing but he does it with the best possible motives as distinct from all the other conspirators, and he fails because he is just not shrewd enough, not clever enough. The play deals with mistakes and it is still very relevant today. If you have been in an office revolution where someone is trying to oust someone else from a position, the ganging up that goes on is exactly the same – not as bloody, but there are the same intrigues, the same justifications. But Brutus is the lynch-pin. Although he is a prig and he's a fool, the spectacle of a man attempting to do good and achieving nothing but the holocaust I find extremely moving. That's what the play is about to me.'

THE BBC TV CAST AND PRODUCTION TEAM

The cast for the BBC television production was as follows:

MARCUS BRUTUS	Richard Pasco
JULIUS CAESAR	Charles Gray
MARCUS ANTONIUS	Keith Michell
CASSIUS	David Collings
PORTIA	Virginia McKenna
CALPHURNIA	Elizabeth Spriggs
CASCA	Sam Dastor
FLAVIUS	John Laurimore
MARULLUS	John Sterland
OCTAVIUS CAESAR	Garrick Hagon
MESSALA	Brian Coburn
TITINIUS	Leonard Preston
DECIUS BRUTUS	Alex Davion
CINNA	Darien Angadi
LUCILIUS	Andrew Hilton
LIGARIUS	Anthony Dawes
METELLUS	Roger Bizley
CICERO	Manning Wilson
SOOTHSAYER	Ronald Forfar
ARTEMIDORUS	Patrick Marley
TREBONIUS	William Simons
CINNA THE POET	John Tordoff
YOUNG CATO	Philip York
CLITUS	Christopher Good
PINDARUS	Robert Oates
1ST CITIZEN/1ST PLEBEIAN	Alan Thompson
2ND CITIZEN/2ND PLEBEIAN	Leo Dolan
3RD PLEBEIAN/1ST SOLDIER	Johnny Wade
4TH PLEBEIAN/2ND SOLDIER	David Henry
LUCIUS	Jonathan Scott-Taylor
CLAUDIUS/ANTONY'S SERVANT	Tom Kelly

OCTAVIUS' SERVANT/MESSENGER	Jack Elliott
CAESAR'S SERVANT	Michael Cogan
POET	Reginald Jessup
STRATO	Maurice Thorogood
VARRO	Michael Greatorex
VOLUMNIUS	Nicholas Gecks
DARDANIUS	Michael Jenkinson
LEPIDUS	Roy Spencer
POPILIUS	Terence Conoley
PUBLIUS	Noel Johnson
FIGHT DIRECTOR	William Hobbs
PRODUCTION ASSISTANT	Diarmuid Lawrence
PRODUCTION UNIT MANAGER	Fraser Lowden
MUSIC	Mike Steer
MUSIC ADVISOR	David Lloyd-Jones
LITERARY CONSULTANT	John Wilders
MAKE-UP ARTIST	Jean Steward
COSTUME DESIGNER	Odette Barrow
SOUND	Chick Anthony
LIGHTING	Howard King
SCRIPT EDITOR	Alan Shallcross
DESIGNER	Tony Abbott
PRODUCER	Cedric Messina
DIRECTOR	Herbert Wise

The production was recorded between 26 and 31 July 1978

THE TEXT

In order to help readers who might wish to use this text to follow the play on the screen the scene divisions and locations used in the television production and any cuts and rearrangements made are shown in the right-hand margins. The principles governing these annotations are as follows:

1. Where a new location (change of set) is used by the TV production this is shown as a new scene. The scenes are numbered consecutively and each one is identified as exterior or interior, located by a brief description of the set or the location, and placed in its 'time' setting (e.g. Day, Night, Dawn). These procedures are those used in BBC Television camera scripts.

2. Where the original stage direction shows the entry of a character at the beginning of a scene, this has not been deleted (unless it causes confusion). This is in order to demonstrate which characters are in the scene, since in most cases the TV scene begins with the characters 'discovered' on the set.

3. Where the start of a TV scene does not coincide with the start of a scene in the printed text, the characters in that scene have been listed, *unless* the start of the scene coincides with a stage direction which indicates the entrance of all those characters.

4. Where the text has been cut in the TV production, the cuts are marked by vertical rules and by a note in the margin. If complete lines are cut, these are shown as, e.g., Lines 27–38 omitted. If part of a line only is cut, or in cases of doubt (e.g. in prose passages), the first and last words of the cut are also given.

5. Occasionally, and only when it is thought necessary for comprehension of the action, a note of a character's moves has been inserted in the margin.

6. Where complete sets are used or where the action moves from one part of a set to another, no attempt has been made to show this as a succession of scenes.

ALAN SHALLCROSS

JULIUS CÆSAR

DRAMATIS PERSONÆ

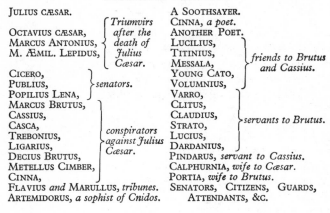

JULIUS CÆSAR.

OCTAVIUS CÆSAR,
MARCUS ANTONIUS,
M. ÆMIL. LEPIDUS, } *Triumvirs after the death of Julius Cæsar.*

CICERO,
PUBLIUS, } *senators.*
POPILIUS LENA,

MARCUS BRUTUS,
CASSIUS,
CASCA,
TREBONIUS,
LIGARIUS,
DECIUS BRUTUS,
METELLUS CIMBER,
CINNA, } *conspirators against Julius Cæsar.*

FLAVIUS and MARULLUS, *tribunes.*
ARTEMIDORUS, *a sophist of Cnidos.*

A SOOTHSAYER.
CINNA, *a poet.*
ANOTHER POET.
LUCILIUS,
TITINIUS,
MESSALA,
YOUNG CATO,
VOLUMNIUS, } *friends to Brutus and Cassius.*

VARRO,
CLITUS,
CLAUDIUS,
STRATO,
LUCIUS,
DARDANIUS, } *servants to Brutus.*

PINDARUS, *servant to Cassius.*
CALPHURNIA, *wife to Cæsar.*
PORTIA, *wife to Brutus.*
SENATORS, CITIZENS, GUARDS,
ATTENDANTS, &C.

THE SCENE: *Rome ; near Sardis ; near Philippi.*

ACT ONE

SCENE I. *Rome. A street.*

SCENE I
*Exterior. Rome.
A Street. Day.*

Enter FLAVIUS, MARULLUS, *and certain* COMMONERS *over the stage.*

FLAV. Hence ! home, you idle creatures, get you home.
    Is this a holiday ? What ! know you not,
    Being mechanical, you ought not walk
    Upon a labouring day without the sign
    Of your profession ? Speak, what trade art thou ?   5
I CIT. Why, sir, a carpenter.
MAR. Where is thy leather apron and thy rule ?
    What dost thou with thy best apparel on ?
    You, sir, what trade are you ?
2 CIT. Truly, sir, in respect of a fine workman, I am but, as you would
    say, a cobbler.   11
MAR. But what trade art thou ? Answer me directly.
2 CIT. A trade, sir, that I hope I may use with a safe conscience, which
    is indeed, sir, a mender of bad soles.
MAR. What trade, thou knave ? Thou naughty knave, what trade ?
2 CIT. Nay, I beseech you, sir, be not out with me ; yet, if you be out,
    sir, I can mend you.
MAR. What mean'st thou by that ? Mend me, thou saucy fellow !

2 CIT. Why, sir, cobble you.   20
FLAV. Thou art a cobbler, art thou ?
2 CIT. Truly, sir, all that I live by is with the awl. I meddle with
no tradesman's matters nor women's matters, but with awl. I am
indeed, sir, a surgeon to old shoes. When they are in great
danger, I re-cover them. As proper men as ever trod upon neat's
leather have gone upon my handiwork.   27
FLAV. But wherefore art not in thy shop to-day ?
Why dost thou lead these men about the streets ?
2 CIT. Truly, sir, to wear out their shoes, to get myself into more
work. But indeed, sir, we make holiday to see Cæsar, and to
rejoice in his triumph.
MAR. Wherefore rejoice ? What conquest brings he home ?
What tributaries follow him to Rome,
To grace in captive bonds his chariot wheels ?   35
You blocks, you stones, you worse than senseless things !
O you hard hearts, you cruel men of Rome,
Knew you not Pompey ? Many a time and oft
Have you climb'd up to walls and battlements,
To tow'rs and windows, yea, to chimney-tops,   40
Your infants in your arms, and there have sat
The livelong day, with patient expectation,
To see great Pompey pass the streets of Rome.
And when you saw his chariot but appear,
Have you not made an universal shout,   45
That Tiber trembled underneath her banks,
To hear the replication of your sounds
Made in her concave shores ?
And do you now put on your best attire ?
And do you now cull out a holiday ?   50
And do you now strew flowers in his way
That comes in triumph over Pompey's blood ?
Be gone !
Run to your houses, fall upon your knees,
Pray to the gods to intermit the plague   55
That needs must light on this ingratitude.
FLAV. Go, go, good countrymen, and for this fault
Assemble all the poor men of your sort ;
Draw them to Tiber banks, and weep your tears
Into the channel, till the lowest stream   60
Do kiss the most exalted shores of all.
                          [Exeunt all the Commoners.
See whe'r their basest metal be not mov'd ;
They vanish tongue-tied in their guiltiness.
Go you down that way towards the Capitol ;
This way will I. Disrobe the images   65
If you do find them deck'd with ceremonies.
MAR. May we do so ?
You know it is the feast of Lupercal.
FLAV. It is no matter ; let no images
Be hung with Cæsar's trophies. I'll about,   70
And drive away the vulgar from the streets ;
So do you too, where you perceive them thick.
These growing feathers pluck'd from Cæsar's wing

Will make him fly an ordinary pitch,
Who else would soar above the view of men,   75
And keep us all in servile fearfulness.   [*Exeunt.*

SCENE II. *Rome. A public place.*

Music. Enter CÆSAR ; ANTONY, *for the course ;* CALPHURNIA, PORTIA,
DECIUS, CICERO, BRUTUS, CASSIUS, *and* CASCA ; *a great crowd
following, among them a* SOOTHSAYER ; *after them,* MARULLUS *and*
FLAVIUS.

SCENE 2
*Exterior. Rome.
A Street. Day.*

CÆS. Calphurnia.
CASCA.   Peace, ho ! Cæsar speaks.   [*Music ceases.*
CÆS. Calphurnia.
CAL. Here, my lord.
CÆS. Stand you directly in Antonius' way
When he doth run his course.   Antonius !
ANT. Cæsar, my lord.   5
CÆS. Forget not in your speed, Antonius,
To touch Calphurnia ; for our elders say,
The barren, touched in this holy chase,
Shake off their sterile curse.
ANT.   I shall remember.
When Cæsar says ' Do this ', it is perform'd.   10
CÆS. Set on, and leave no ceremony out.   [*Music.*
SOOTH. Cæsar !
CÆS. Ha ! Who calls ?
CASCA. Bid every noise be still.   Peace yet again.   [*Music ceases.*
CÆS. Who is it in the press that calls on me ?   15
I hear a tongue, shriller than all the music,
Cry ' Cæsar ! ' Speak.   Cæsar is turn'd to hear.
SOOTH. Beware the ides of March.
CÆS.   What man is that ?
BRU. A soothsayer bids you beware the ides of March.
CÆS. Set him before me ; let me see his face.   20
CAS. Fellow, come from the throng ; look upon Cæsar.
CÆS. What say'st thou to me now ?   Speak once again.
SOOTH. Beware the ides of March.
CÆS. He is a dreamer ; let us leave him.   Pass.
                    [*Sennet.   Exeunt all but* BRUTUS *and* CASSIUS.
CAS. Will you go see the order of the course ?   25
BRU. Not I.
CAS. I pray you do.
BRU. I am not gamesome : I do lack some part
Of that quick spirit that is in Antony.
Let me not hinder, Cassius, your desires ;   30
I'll leave you.
CAS. Brutus, I do observe you now of late ;
I have not from your eyes that gentleness
And show of love as I was wont to have.
You bear too stubborn and too strange a hand   35
Over your friend that loves you.
BRU.   Cassius,
Be not deceiv'd.   If I have veil'd my look,
I turn the trouble of my countenance

33

Merely upon myself. Vexed I am
Of late with passions of some difference,   40
Conceptions only proper to myself,
Which give some soil, perhaps, to my behaviours ;
But let not therefore my good friends be griev'd—
Among which number, Cassius, be you one—
Nor construe any further my neglect   45
Than that poor Brutus, with himself at war,
Forgets the shows of love to other men.
CAS. Then, Brutus, I have much mistook your passion,
By means whereof this breast of mine hath buried
Thoughts of great value, worthy cogitations.   50
Tell me, good Brutus, can you see your face ?
BRU. No, Cassius ; for the eye sees not itself
But by reflection, by some other things.
CAS. 'Tis just ;
And it is very much lamented, Brutus,   55
That you have no such mirrors as will turn
Your hidden worthiness into your eye,
That you might see your shadow.   I have heard,
Where many of the best respect in Rome—
Except immortal Cæsar—speaking of Brutus,   60
And groaning underneath this age's yoke,
Have wish'd that noble Brutus had his eyes.
BRU. Into what dangers would you lead me, Cassius,
That you would have me seek into myself
For that which is not in me ?   65
CAS. Therefore, good Brutus, be prepar'd to hear ;
And since you know you cannot see yourself
So well as by reflection, I, your glass,
Will modestly discover to yourself
That of yourself which you yet know not of.   70
And be not jealous on me, gentle Brutus :
Were I a common laughter, or did use
To stale with ordinary oaths my love
To every new protester ; if you know
That I do fawn on men and hug them hard,   75
And after scandal them ; or if you know
That I profess myself in banqueting
To all the rout, then hold me dangerous.   [Flourish and shout.
BRU. What means this shouting ?   I do fear the people
Choose Cæsar for their king.
CAS.   Ay, do you fear it ?   80
Then must I think you would not have it so.
BRU. I would not, Cassius ; yet I love him well.
But wherefore do you hold me here so long ?
What is it that you would impart to me ?
If it be aught toward the general good,   85
Set honour in one eye and death i' th' other,
And I will look on both indifferently ;
For let the gods so speed me as I love
The name of honour more than I fear death.
CAS. I know that virtue to be in you, Brutus,   90
As well as I do know your outward favour.

34

Well, honour is the subject of my story.
I cannot tell what you and other men
Think of this life ; but, for my single self,
I had as lief not be as live to be   95
In awe of such a thing as I myself.
I was born free as Cæsar ; so were you.
We both have fed as well, and we can both
Endure the winter's cold as well as he.
For once, upon a raw and gusty day,   100
The troubled Tiber chafing with her shores,
Cæsar said to me ' Dar'st thou, Cassius, now
Leap in with me into this angry flood,
And swim to yonder point ? ' Upon the word,
Accoutred as I was, I plunged in   105
And bade him follow.   So indeed he did.
The torrent roar'd, and we did buffet it
With lusty sinews, throwing it aside
And stemming it with hearts of controversy ;
But ere we could arrive the point propos'd,   110
Cæsar cried ' Help me, Cassius, or I sink ! '
I, as Æneas, our great ancestor,
Did from the flames of Troy upon his shoulder
The old Anchises bear, so from the waves of Tiber
Did I the tired Cæsar.   And this man   115
Is now become a god ; and Cassius is
A wretched creature, and must bend his body
If Cæsar carelessly but nod on him.
He had a fever when he was in Spain,
And when the fit was on him I did mark   120
How he did shake.   'Tis true, this god did shake.
His coward lips did from their colour fly,
And that same eye, whose bend doth awe the world,
Did lose his lustre.   I did hear him groan.
Ay, and that tongue of his, that bade the Romans   125
Mark him, and write his speeches in their books,
Alas ! it cried ' Give me some drink, Titinius '
As a sick girl.   Ye gods ! it doth amaze me
A man of such a feeble temper should
So get the start of the majestic world,   130
And bear the palm alone.   [*Shout.   Flourish.*
BRU. Another general shout !
I do believe that these applauses are
For some new honours that are heap'd on Cæsar.
CAS. Why, man, he doth bestride the narrow world   135
Like a Colossus, and we petty men
Walk under his huge legs, and peep about
To find ourselves dishonourable graves.
Men at some time are masters of their fates :
The fault, dear Brutus, is not in our stars,   140
But in ourselves, that we are underlings.
' Brutus ' and ' Cæsar '.   What should be in that ' Cæsar ' ?
Why should that name be sounded more than yours ?
Write them together ; yours is as fair a name.
Sound them : it doth become the mouth as well.   145

Weigh them : it is as heavy.   Conjure with 'em :
' Brutus ' will start a spirit as soon as ' Cæsar '.
Now, in the names of all the gods at once,
Upon what meat doth this our Cæsar feed,
That he is grown so great ?   Age, thou art sham'd !   150
Rome, thou has lost the breed of noble bloods !
When went there by an age, since the great flood,
But it was fam'd with more than with one man ?
When could they say, till now, that talk'd of Rome,
That her wide walls encompass'd but one man ?   155
Now is it Rome indeed, and room enough,
When there is in it but one only man.
O ! you and I have heard our fathers say
There was a Brutus once that would have brook'd
Th' eternal devil to keep his state in Rome   160
As easily as a king.
BRU. That you do love me, I am nothing jealous ;
What you would work me to, I have some aim ;
How I have thought of this, and of these times,
I shall recount hereafter.   For this present,   165
I would not, so with love I might entreat you,
Be any further mov'd.   What you have said
I will consider ; what you have to say
I will with patience hear ; and find a time
Both meet to hear and answer such high things.   170
Till then, my noble friend, chew upon this :
Brutus had rather be a villager
Than to repute himself a son of Rome
Under these hard conditions as this time
Is like to lay upon us.   175
CAS. I am glad that my weak words
Have struck but thus much show of fire from Brutus.

Re-enter CÆSAR *and his* TRAIN.

BRU. The games are done, and Cæsar is returning.
CAS. As they pass by, pluck Casca by the sleeve,
And he will, after his sour fashion, tell you   180
What hath proceeded worthy note to-day.
BRU. I will do so.   But, look you, Cassius,
The angry spot doth glow on Cæsar's brow,
And all the rest look like a chidden train ;
Calphurnia's cheek is pale, and Cicero   185
Looks with such ferret and such fiery eyes
As we have seen him in the Capitol,
Being cross'd in conference by some senators.
CAS. Casca will tell us what the matter is.
CÆS. Antonius !   190
ANT. Cæsar ?
CÆS. Let me have men about me that are fat ;
Sleek-headed men, and such as sleep o' nights.
Yond Cassius has a lean and hungry look ;
He thinks too much.   Such men are dangerous.   195
ANT. Fear him not, Cæsar, he's not dangerous ;
He is a noble Roman, and well given.

CÆS. Would he were fatter ! But I fear him not.
Yet if my name were liable to fear,
I do not know the man I should avoid   200
So soon as that spare Cassius. He reads much,
He is a great observer, and he looks
Quite through the deeds of men. He loves no plays,
As thou dost, Antony ; he hears no music.
Seldom he smiles, and smiles in such a sort   205
As if he mock'd himself, and scorn'd his spirit
That could be mov'd to smile at anything.
Such men as he be never at heart's ease
Whiles they behold a greater than themselves,
And therefore are they very dangerous.   210
I rather tell thee what is to be fear'd
Than what I fear ; for always I am Cæsar.
Come on my right hand, for this ear is deaf,
And tell me truly what thou think'st of him.
                    [Sennet. Exeunt CÆSAR and his TRAIN.
| CASCA. You pull'd me by the cloak. Would you speak with me ? | 'You pull'd me by the
BRU. Ay, Casca ; tell us what hath chanc'd to-day,   216   cloak' omitted.
    That Cæsar looks so sad ?
CASCA. Why, you were with him, were you not ?
BRU. I should not then ask Casca what had chanc'd.
CASCA. Why, there was a crown offer'd him ; and being offer'd him,
    he put it by with the back of his hand, thus ; and then the people
    fell a-shouting.
BRU. What was the second noise for ?
CASCA. Why, for that too.
CAS. They shouted thrice ; what was the last cry for ?   225
CASCA. Why, for that too.
BRU. Was the crown offer'd him thrice ?
CASCA. Ay, marry, was't, and he put it by thrice, every time gentler
    than other ; and at every putting by mine honest neighbours
    shouted.   230
CAS. Who offer'd him the crown ?
CASCA. Why, Antony.
BRU. Tell us the manner of it, gentle Casca.
CASCA. I can as well be hang'd as tell the manner of it : it was mere
    foolery ; I did not mark it. I saw Mark Antony offer him a crown
    yet 'twas not a crown neither, 'twas one of these coronets—and,
    as I told you, he put it by once ; but for all that, to my thinking,
    he would fain have had it. Then he offered it to him again ; then
    he put it by again ; but to my thinking, he was very loath to lay
    his fingers off it. And then he offered it the third time ; he put
    it the third time by ; and still as he refus'd it, the rabblement
    hooted, and clapp'd their chopt hands, and threw up their sweaty
    night-caps, and uttered such a deal of stinking breath because
    Cæsar refus'd the crown, that it had almost choked Cæsar ; for
    he swooned and fell down at it. And for mine own part I durst
    not laugh, for fear of opening my lips and receiving the bad air.
CAS. But soft, I pray you. What, did Cæsar swoon ?   250
CASCA. He fell down in the market-place, and foam'd at mouth, and
    was speechless.
BRU. 'Tis very like. He hath the falling sickness.

CAS. No, Cæsar hath it not ; but you, and I,
And honest Casca, we have the falling sickness.   255
CASCA. I know not what you mean by that, but I am sure Cæsar fell
down.   If the tag-rag people did not clap him and hiss him,
according as he pleas'd and displeas'd them, as they use to do the
players in the theatre, I am no true man.   260
BRU. What said he when he came unto himself?
CASCA. Marry, before he fell down, when he perceiv'd the common
herd was glad he refus'd the crown, he pluckt me ope his doublet,
and offer'd them his throat to cut.   An I had been a man of any
occupation, if I would not have taken him at a word, I would I
might go to hell among the rogues.   And so he fell.   When he
came to himself again, he said, if he had done or said anything
amiss, he desir'd their worships to think it was his infirmity.
Three or four wenches, where I stood, cried ' Alas, good soul ! '
and forgave him with all their hearts.   But there's no heed to be
taken of them ; if Cæsar had stabb'd their mothers, they would
have done no less.   274
BRU. And after that, he came thus sad away ?
CASCA. Ay.
CAS. Did Cicero say anything ?
CASCA. Ay, he spoke Greek.
CAS. To what effect ?
CASCA. Nay, an I tell you that, I'll ne'er look you i' th' face again.
But those that understood him smil'd at one another, and shook
their heads ; but for mine own part, it was Greek to me.   I could
tell you more news too : Marullus and Flavius, for pulling scarfs
off Cæsar's images, are put to silence.   Fare you well.   There
was more foolery yet, if I could remember it.   286
CAS. Will you sup with me to-night, Casca ?
CASCA. No, I am promis'd forth.
CAS. Will you dine with me to-morrow ?
CASCA. Ay, if I be alive, and your mind hold, and your dinner worth
the eating.   291
CAS. Good ; I will expect you.
CASCA. Do so.   Farewell, both.   [Exit.
BRU. What a blunt fellow is this grown to be !
He was quick mettle when he went to school.   295
CAS. So is he now, in execution
Of any bold or noble enterprise,
However he puts on this tardy form.
This rudeness is a sauce to his good wit,
Which gives men stomach to digest his words   300
With better appetite.
BRU. And so it is.   For this time I will leave you.
To-morrow, if you please to speak with me,
I will come home to you ; or, if you will,
Come home to me, and I will wait for you.   305
CAS. I will do so.   Till then, think of the world.   [Exit BRUTUS.
Well, Brutus, thou art noble ; yet, I see,
Thy honourable metal may be wrought
From that it is dispos'd.   Therefore it is meet
That noble minds keep ever with their likes ;   310
For who so firm that cannot be seduc'd ?

Cæsar doth bear me hard ; but he loves Brutus.
If I were Brutus now and he were Cassius,
He should not humour me. I will this night,
In several hands, in at his windows throw,   315
As if they came from several citizens,
Writings, all tending to the great opinion
That Rome holds of his name ; wherein obscurely
Cæsar's ambition shall be glanced at.
And, after this, let Cæsar seat him sure ;   320
For we will shake him, or worse days endure.   [Exit.

SCENE III. Rome. A street.

*Thunder and lightning. Enter, from opposite sides, CASCA,
with his sword drawn, and CICERO.*

SCENE 3
Exterior. Rome.
A Street. Night.

CIC. Good even, Casca. Brought you Cæsar home ?
Why are you breathless ? and why stare you so ?
CASCA. Are not you mov'd, when all the sway of earth
Shakes like a thing unfirm ? O Cicero,
I have seen tempests when the scolding winds   5
Have riv'd the knotty oaks, and I have seen
Th' ambitious ocean swell, and rage, and foam,
To be exalted with the threat'ning clouds ;
But never till to-night, never till now,
Did I go through a tempest dropping fire.   10
Either there is a civil strife in heaven,
Or else the world, too saucy with the gods,
Incenses them to send destruction.
CIC. Why, saw you anything more wonderful ?
CASCA. A common slave—you know him well by sight—   15
Held up his left hand, which did flame and burn
Like twenty torches join'd ; and yet his hand,
Not sensible of fire, remain'd unscorch'd.
Besides—I ha' not since put up my sword—
Against the Capitol I met a lion,   20
Who glar'd upon me, and went surly by
Without annoying me ; and there were drawn
Upon a heap a hundred ghastly women,
Transformed with their fear, who swore they saw
Men, all in fire, walk up and down the streets.   25
And yesterday the bird of night did sit,
Even at noon-day, upon the market-place,
Hooting and shrieking. When these prodigies
Do so conjointly meet, let not men say
' These are their reasons—they are natural ',   30
For I believe they are portentous things
Unto the climate that they point upon.
CIC. Indeed, it is a strange-disposed time ;
But men may construe things after their fashion,
Clean from the purpose of the things themselves.   35
Comes Cæsar to the Capitol to-morrow ?
CASCA. He doth ; for he did bid Antonius
Send word to you he would be there to-morrow.

39

CIC. Good night, then, Casca ; this disturbed sky
  Is not to walk in.
CASCA.   Farewell, Cicero.   [*Exit* CICERO.

Enter CASSIUS.

CAS. Who's there ?
CASCA.   A Roman.
CAS.   Casca, by your voice.
CASCA. Your ear is good.   Cassius, what night is this !
CAS. A very pleasing night to honest men.
CASCA. Who ever knew the heavens menace so ?
CAS. Those that have known the earth so full of faults.   45
  For my part, I have walk'd about the streets,
  Submitting me unto the perilous night,
  And, thus unbraced, Casca, as you see,
  Have bar'd my bosom to the thunderstone ;
  And when the cross blue lightning seem'd to open   50
  The breast of heaven, I did present myself
  Even in the aim and very flash of it.
CASCA. But wherefore did you so much tempt the heavens ?
  It is the part of men to fear and tremble
  When the most mighty gods by tokens send   55
  Such dreadful heralds to astonish us.
CAS. You are dull, Casca, and those sparks of life
  That should be in a Roman you do want,
  Or else you use not.   You look pale, and gaze,
  And put on fear, and cast yourself in wonder,   60
  To see the strange impatience of the heavens ;
  But if you would consider the true cause—
  Why all these fires, why all these gliding ghosts,
  Why birds and beasts, from quality and kind ;
  Why old men, fools, and children calculate;   65
  Why all these things change from their ordinance,
  Their natures and preformed faculties,
  To monstrous quality—why, you shall find
  That heaven hath infus'd them with these spirits,
  To make them instruments of fear and warning   70
  Unto some monstrous state.
  Now could I, Casca, name to thee a man
  Most like this dreadful night
  That thunders, lightens, opens graves, and roars
  As doth the lion in the Capitol ;   75
  A man no mightier than thyself or me
  In personal action, yet prodigious grown,
  And fearful, as these strange eruptions are.
CASCA. 'Tis Cæsar that you mean, is it not, Cassius ?
CAS. Let it be who it is ; for Romans now   80
  Have thews and limbs like to their ancestors.
  But woe the while ! our fathers' minds are dead,
  And we are govern'd with our mothers' spirits ;
  Our yoke and sufferance show us womanish.
CASCA. Indeed they say the senators to-morrow   85
  Mean to establish Cæsar as a king ;
  And he shall wear his crown by sea and land,

In every place save here in Italy.
CAS. I know where I will wear this dagger then;
   Cassius from bondage will deliver Cassius.   90
   Therein, ye gods, you make the weak most strong
   Therein, ye gods, you tyrants do defeat.
   Nor stony tower, nor walls of beaten brass,
   Nor airless dungeon, nor strong links of iron,
   Can be retentive to the strength of spirit;   95
   But life, being weary of these worldly bars,
   Never lacks power to dismiss itself.
   If I know this, know all the world besides,
   That part of tyranny that I do bear,
   I can shake off at pleasure.   *[Thunder still.*
CASCA.   So can I;   100
   So every bondman in his own hand bears
   The power to cancel his captivity.
CAS. And why should Cæsar be a tyrant, then?
   Poor man! I know he would not be a wolf
   But that he sees the Romans are but sheep;   105
   He were no lion, were not Romans hinds.
   Those that with haste will make a mighty fire
   Begin it with weak straws. What trash is Rome,
   What rubbish, and what offal, when it serves
   For the base matter to illuminate   110
   So vile a thing as Cæsar! But, O grief,
   Where hast thou led me? I perhaps speak this
   Before a willing bondman; then I know
   My answer must be made. But I am arm'd,
   And dangers are to me indifferent.   115
CASCA. You speak to Casca, and to such a man
   That is no fleering tell-tale. Hold, my hand.
   Be factious for redress of all these griefs,
   And I will set this foot of mine as far
   As who goes farthest.
CAS.   There's a bargain made.   120
   Now know you, Casca, I have mov'd already
   Some certain of the noblest-minded Romans
   To undergo with me an enterprise
   Of honourable-dangerous consequence;
   And I do know by this they stay for me   125
   In Pompey's porch; for now, this fearful night,
   There is no stir or walking in the streets,
   And the complexion of the element
   In favour's like the work we have in hand,
   Most bloody, fiery, and most terrible.   130

Enter CINNA.

CASCA. Stand close awhile, for here comes one in haste.
CAS. 'Tis Cinna, I do know him by his gait;
   He is a friend. Cinna, where haste you so?
CIN. To find out you. Who's that? Metellus Cimber?
CAS. No, it is Casca, one incorporate   135
   To our attempts. Am I not stay'd for, Cinna?
CIN. I am glad on't. What a fearful night is this!

There's two or three of us have seen strange sights.
CAS. Am I not stay'd for ? Tell me.
CIN. Yes, you are. O Cassius, if you could   140
    But win the noble Brutus to our party—
CAS. Be you content. Good Cinna, take this paper,
    And look you lay it in the prætor's chair,
    Where Brutus may but find it ; and throw this
    In at his window ; set this up with wax   145
    Upon old Brutus' statue. All this done,
    Repair to Pompey's porch, where you shall find us.
    Is Decius Brutus and Trebonius there ?
CIN. All but Metellus Cimber, and he's gone
    To seek you at your house. Well, I will hie,   150
    And so bestow these papers as you bade me.
CAS. That done, repair to Pompey's theatre.   [*Exit* CINNA.
    Come, Casca, you and I will yet ere day
    See Brutus at his house. Three parts of him
    Is ours already, and the man entire   155
    Upon the next encounter yields him ours.
CASCA. O, he sits high in all the people's hearts ;
    And that which would appear offence in us
    His countenance, like richest alchemy,
    Will change to virtue and to worthiness.   160
CAS. Him and his worth and our great need of him
    You have right well conceited. Let us go,
    For it is after midnight ; and ere day
    We will awake him and be sure of him.   [*Exeunt.*

ACT TWO

SCENE I. *Rome.*

Enter BRUTUS *in his orchard.*

BRU. What, Lucius, ho !
    I cannot by the progress of the stars
    Give guess how near to day. Lucius, I say !
    I would it were my fault to sleep so soundly.
    When, Lucius, when ? Awake, I say ! What, Lucius !   5

Enter LUCIUS.

LUC. Call'd you, my lord ?
BRU. Get me a taper in my study, Lucius ;
    When it is lighted, come and call me here.
LUC. I will, my lord.   [*Exit.*
BRU. It must be by his death ; and for my part,   10
    I know no personal cause to spurn at him,
    But for the general : he would be crown'd.
    How that might change his nature, there's the question.
    It is the bright day that brings forth the adder,
    And that craves wary walking. Crown him—that I   15
    And then, I grant, we put a sting in him
    That at his will he may do danger with.
    Th' abuse of greatness is, when it disjoins

SCENE 4
Exterior. Brutus' House.
The Orchard. Night.

Remorse from power ; and to speak truth of Cæsar,
I have not known when his affections sway'd   20
More than his reason.   But 'tis a common proof
That lowliness is young ambition's ladder,
Whereto the climber-upward turns his face ;
But when he once attains the upmost round,
He then unto the ladder turns his back,   25
Looks in the clouds, scorning the base degrees
By which he did ascend.   So Cæsar may.
Then, lest he may, prevent.   And since the quarrel
Will bear no colour for the thing he is,
Fashion it thus—that what he is, augmented,   30
Would run to these and these extremities ;
And therefore think him as a serpent's egg,
Which, hatch'd, would as his kind grow mischievous,
And kill him in the shell.

Re-enter LUCIUS.

LUC. The taper burneth in your closet, sir.   35
  Searching the window for a flint, I found
  This paper, thus seal'd up ; and I am sure
  It did not lie there when I went to bed.   [*Giving him a letter.*
BRU. Get you to bed again, it is not day.
  Is not to-morrow, boy, the ides of March ?   40
LUC. I know not, sir.
BRU. Look in the calendar, and bring me word.
LUC. I will, sir.   [*Exit.*
BRU. The exhalations, whizzing in the air, | Lines 44–45 omitted.
  Give so much light that I may read by them.   45 |
                                        [*Opens the letter and reads.*
' Brutus, thou sleep'st.   Awake, and see thyself.
Shall Rome, &c.   Speak, strike, redress !
Brutus, thou sleep'st ; awake.'
Such instigations have been often dropp'd
Where I have took them up.   50
' Shall Rome, &c.'   Thus must I piece it out :
Shall Rome stand under one man's awe ?   What, Rome ?
My ancestors did from the streets of Rome
The Tarquin drive, when he was call'd a king.
' Speak, strike, redress ! '   Am I entreated   55
To speak and strike ?   O Rome, I make thee promise,
If the redress will follow, thou receivest
Thy full petition at the hand of Brutus !

Re-enter LUCIUS.

LUC. Sir, March is wasted fifteen days.   [*Knocking within.*
BRU. 'Tis good.   Go to the gate ; somebody knocks.   [*Exit* LUCIUS.
  Since Cassius first did whet me against Cæsar,
  I have not slept.
  Between the acting of a dreadful thing
  And the first motion, all the interim is
  Like a phantasma or a hideous dream.   65
  The Genius and the mortal instruments
  Are then in council ; and the state of man,

Like to a little kingdom, suffers then
The nature of an insurrection.

Re-enter LUCIUS.

LUC. Sir, 'tis your brother Cassius at the door   70
Who doth desire to see you.
BRU.   Is he alone?
LUC. No, sir, there are more with him.
BRU.   Do you know them?
LUC. No, sir; their hats are pluck'd about their ears
And half their faces buried in their cloaks,
That by no means I may discover them   75
By any mark of favour.
BRU.   Let 'em enter.   [*Exit* LUCIUS.
They are the faction. O conspiracy,
Sham'st thou to show thy dang'rous brow by night,
When evils are most free? O, then by day
Where wilt thou find a cavern dark enough   80
To mask thy monstrous visage? Seek none, conspiracy;
Hide it in smiles and affability!
For if thou hath thy native semblance on,
Not Erebus itself were dim enough
To hide thee from prevention.   85

Enter the conspirators, CASSIUS, CASCA, DECIUS, CINNA,
METELLUS CIMBER, *and* TREBONIUS.

CAS. I think we are too bold upon your rest.
Good morrow, Brutus.   Do we trouble you?
BRU. I have been up this hour, awake all night.
Know I these men that come along with you?
CAS. Yes, every man of them; and no man here   90
But honours you; and every one doth wish
You had but that opinion of yourself
Which every noble Roman bears of you.
This is Trebonius.
BRU.   He is welcome hither.
CAS. This, Decius Brutus.
BRU.   He is welcome too.   95
CAS. This, Casca; this, Cinna;
And this, Metellus Cimber.
BRU.   They are all welcome.
What watchful cares do interpose themselves
Betwixt your eyes and night?
CAS. Shall I entreat a word?   [*They whisper.*
DEC. Here lies the east.   Doth not the day break here?
CASCA. No.
CIN. O, pardon, sir, it doth; and yon grey lines
That fret the clouds are messengers of day.
CASCA. You shall confess that you are both deceiv'd.   105
Here, as I point my sword, the sun arises;
Which is a great way growing on the south,
Weighing the youthful season of the year.
Some two months hence up higher toward the north
He first presents his fire; and the high east   110

Stands as the Capitol, directly here.
BRU. Give me your hands all over, one by one.
CAS. And let us swear our resolution.
BRU. No, not an oath. If not the face of men,
The sufferance of our souls, the time's abuse,   115
If these be motives weak, break off betimes,
And every man hence to his idle bed.
So let high-sighted tyranny range on,
Till each man drop by lottery. But if these,
As I am sure they do, bear fire enough   120
To kindle cowards, and to steel with valour
The melting spirits of women, then, countrymen,
What need we any spur but our own cause
To prick us to redress ? What other bond
Than secret Romans that have spoke the word   125
And will not palter ? And what other oath
Than honesty to honesty engag'd
That this shall be or we will fall for it ?
Swear priests and cowards and men cautelous,
Old feeble carrions and such suffering souls   130
That welcome wrongs ; unto bad causes swear
Such creatures as men doubt ; but do not stain
The even virtue of our enterprise,
Nor th' insuppressive mettle of our spirits,
To think that or our cause or our performance   135
Did need an oath ; when every drop of blood
That every Roman bears, and nobly bears,
Is guilty of a several bastardy,
If he do break the smallest particle
Of any promise that hath pass'd from him.   140
CAS. But what of Cicero ? Shall we sound him ?
I think he will stand very strong with us.
CASCA. Let us not leave him out.
CIN.   No, by no means.
MET. O, let us have him ; for his silver hairs
Will purchase us a good opinion,   145
And buy men's voices to commend our deeds.
It shall be said his judgment rul'd our hands ;
Our youths and wildness shall no whit appear,
But all be buried in his gravity.
BRU. O, name him not ! Let us not break with him ;   150
For he will never follow any thing
That other men begin.
CAS.   Then leave him out.
CASCA. Indeed he is not fit.
DEC. Shall no man else be touch'd but only Cæsar ?
CAS. Decius, well urg'd. I think it is not meet   155
Mark Antony, so well belov'd of Cæsar,
Should outlive Cæsar. We shall find of him
A shrewd contriver ; and you know his means,
If he improve them, may well stretch so far
As to annoy us all ; which to prevent,   160
Let Antony and Cæsar fall together.
BRU. Our course will seem too bloody, Caius Cassius,

45

To cut the head off and then hack the limbs—
Like wrath in death and envy afterwards ;
For Antony is but a limb of Cæsar.   165
Let's be sacrificers, but not butchers, Caius.
We all stand up against the spirit of Cæsar,
And in the spirit of men there is no blood.
O that we then could come by Cæsar's spirit,
And not dismember Cæsar ! But, alas,   170
Cæsar must bleed for it ! And, gentle friends,
Let's kill him boldly, but not wrathfully ;
Let's carve him as a dish fit for the gods,
Not hew him as a carcase fit for hounds ;
And let our hearts, as subtle masters do,   175
Stir up their servants to an act of rage,
And after seem to chide 'em. This shall make
Our purpose necessary, and not envious ;
Which so appearing to the common eyes
We shall be call'd purgers, not murderers.   180
And for Mark Antony, think not of him ;
For he can do no more than Cæsar's arm
When Cæsar's head is off.
CAS.   Yet I fear him ;
For in the engrafted love he bears to Cæsar—
BRU. Alas, good Cassius, do not think of him !   185
If he love Cæsar, all that he can do
Is to himself take thought and die for Cæsar ;
And that were much he should, for he is given
To sports, to wildness, and much company.
TREB. There is no fear in him. Let him not die ;   190
For he will live, and laugh at this hereafter.   [*Clock strikes.*
BRU. Peace ! Count the clock.
CAS.   The clock hath stricken three.
TREB. 'Tis time to part.
CAS.   But it is doubtful yet
Whether Cæsar will come forth to-day or no ;
For he is superstitious grown of late,   195
Quite from the main opinion he held once
Of fantasy, of dreams, and ceremonies.
It may be these apparent prodigies,
The unaccustom'd terror of this night,
And the persuasion of his augurers,   200
May hold him from the Capitol to-day.
DEC. Never fear that. If he be so resolv'd,
I can o'ersway him ; for he loves to hear
That unicorns may be betray'd with trees,
And bears with glasses, elephants with holes.   205
Lions with toils, and men with flatterers ;
But when I tell him he hates flatterers,
He says he does, being then most flattered.
Let me work ;
For I can give his humour the true bent,   210
And I will bring him to the Capitol.
CAS. Nay, we will all of us be there to fetch him.
BRU. By the eighth hour. Is that the uttermost ?

CIN. Be that the uttermost, and fail not then.
MET. Caius Ligarius doth bear Cæsar hard, 215
  Who rated him for speaking well of Pompey.
  I wonder none of you have thought of him.
BRU. Now, good Metellus, go along by him.
  He loves me well, and I have given him reasons;
  Send him but hither, and I'll fashion him. 220
CAS. The morning comes upon's. We'll leave you, Brutus.
  And, friends, disperse yourselves ; but all remember
  What you have said, and show yourselves true Romans.
BRU. Good gentlemen, look fresh and merrily ;
  Let not our looks put on our purposes, 225
  But bear it as our Roman actors do,
  With untir'd spirits and formal constancy.
  And so good morrow to you every one. [Exeunt all but BRUTUS.
  Boy ! Lucius ! Fast asleep ? It is no matter ;
  Enjoy the honey-heavy dew of slumber. 230
  Thou hast no figures nor no fantasies
  Which busy care draws in the brains of men ;
  Therefore thou sleep'st so sound.

BRUTUS enters the house, sees LUCIUS and returns to the orchard where PORTIA joins him.

Enter PORTIA.

POR. Brutus, my lord !
BRU. Portia, what mean you ? Wherefore rise you now ?
  It is not for your health thus to commit 235
  Your weak condition to the raw cold morning.
POR. Nor for yours neither. Y'have ungently, Brutus,
  Stole from my bed ; and yesternight at supper
  You suddenly arose and walk'd about,
  Musing and sighing, with your arms across ; 240
  And when I ask'd you what the matter was,
  You star'd upon me with ungentle looks.
  I urg'd you further ; then you scratch'd your head
  And too impatiently stamp'd with your foot.
  Yet I insisted ; yet you answer'd not, 245
  But with an angry wafture of your hand
  Gave sign for me to leave you. So I did,
  Fearing to strengthen that impatience
  Which seem'd too much enkindled; and withal
  Hoping it was but an effect of humour, 250
  Which sometime hath his hour with every man.
  It will not let you eat, nor talk, nor sleep ;
  And, could it work so much upon your shape
  As it hath much prevail'd on your condition,
  I should not know you Brutus. Dear my lord, 255
  Make me acquainted with your cause of grief.
BRU. I am not well in health, and that is all.
POR. Brutus is wise, and, were he not in health,
  He would embrace the means to come by it.
BRU. Why, so I do. Good Portia, go to bed. 260
POR. Is Brutus sick, and is it physical
  To walk unbraced and suck up the humours
  Of the dank morning ? What, is Brutus sick,
  And will he steal out of his wholesome bed,

To dare the vile contagion of the night,   265
And tempt the rheumy and unpurged air
To add unto his sickness ?   No, my Brutus ;
You have some sick offence within your mind,
Which by the right and virtue of my place
I ought to know of ; and upon my knees   270
I charm you, by my once-commended beauty,
By all your vows of love, and that great vow
Which did incorporate and make us one,
That you unfold to me, your self, your half,
Why you are heavy—and what men to-night   275
Have had resort to you ; for here have been
Some six or seven, who did hide their faces
Even from darkness.
BRU.   Kneel not, gentle Portia.
POR. I should not need, if you were gentle Brutus.
Within the bond of marriage, tell me, Brutus,   280
Is it excepted I should know no secrets
That appertain to you ?   Am I your self
But, as it were, in sort or limitation ?
To keep with you at meals, comfort your bed,
And talk to you sometimes ?   Dwell I but in the suburbs
Of your good pleasure ?   If it be no more,   286
Portia is Brutus' harlot, not his wife.
BRU. You are my true and honourable wife,
As dear to me as are the ruddy drops
That visit my sad heart.   290
POR. If this were true, then should I know this secret.
I grant I am a woman ; but withal
A woman that Lord Brutus took to wife.
I grant I am a woman ; but withal
A woman well reputed, Cato's daughter.   295
Think you I am no stronger than my sex,
Being so father'd and so husbanded ?
Tell me your counsels, I will not disclose 'em.
I have made strong proof of my constancy,
Giving myself a voluntary wound   300
Here, in the thigh.   Can I bear that with patience,
And not my husband's secrets ?
BRU.   O ye gods,
Render me worthy of this noble wife !   [*Knocking within.*
Hark, hark ! one knocks.   Portia, go in awhile,
And by and by thy bosom shall partake   305
The secrets of my heart.
All my engagements I will construe to thee,
All the charactery of my sad brows.
Leave me with haste.   [*Exit* PORTIA.   BRUTUS *and* PORTIA
        Lucius, who's that knocks ?   *return to the house and*
                                                              PORTIA *retires.*
            Enter LUCIUS *and* LIGARIUS.

LUC. Here is a sick man that would speak with you.   310
BRU. Caius Ligarius, that Metellus spake of.
    Boy, stand aside.   Caius Ligarius, how ?
LIG. Vouchsafe good morrow from a feeble tongue.

BRU. O, what a time have you chose out, brave Caius,
To wear a kerchief! Would you were not sick!   315
LIG. I am not sick, if Brutus have in hand
Any exploit worthy the name of honour.
BRU. Such an exploit have I in hand, Ligarius,
Had you a healthful ear to hear of it.
LIG. By all the gods that Romans bow before,   320
I here discard my sickness. [*Pulls off his kerchief.*] Soul of Rome!
Brave son, deriv'd from honourable loins!
Thou, like an exorcist, hast conjur'd up
My mortified spirit. Now bid me run,
And I will strive with things impossible;   325
Yea, get the better of them. What's to do?
BRU. A piece of work that will make sick men whole.
LIG. But are not some whole that we must make sick?
BRU. That must we also. What it is, my Caius,
I shall unfold to thee, as we are going,   330
To whom it must be done.
LIG.   Set on your foot,
And with a heart new-fir'd I follow you
To do I know not what; but it sufficeth
That Brutus leads me on.   [*Thunder.*
BRU.   Follow me, then.   [*Exeunt.*

SCENE II. *Rome. Cæsar's house.*

Thunder and lightning.   Enter JULIUS CÆSAR *in his night-gown.*

CÆS. Nor heaven nor earth have been at peace to-night.
Thrice hath Calphurnia in her sleep cried out
'Help, ho! They murder Cæsar!' Who's within?

Enter a SERVANT.

SERV. My lord?
CÆS. Go bid the priests do present sacrifice,   5
And bring me their opinions of success.
SERV. I will, my lord.   [*Exit.*

Enter CALPHURNIA.

CAL. What mean you, Cæsar? Think you to walk forth?
You shall not stir out of your house to-day.
CÆS. Cæsar shall forth; the things that threaten'd me   10
Ne'er look'd but on my back. When they shall see
The face of Cæsar, they are vanished.
CAL. Cæsar, I never stood on ceremonies,
Yet now they fright me. There is one within,
Besides the things that we have heard and seen,   15
Recounts most horrid sights seen by the watch.
A lioness hath whelped in the streets,
And graves have yawn'd and yielded up their dead;
Fierce fiery warriors fight upon the clouds,
In ranks and squadrons and right form of war,   20
Which drizzled blood upon the Capitol;
The noise of battle hurtled in the air;

SCENE 5
*Interior. Caesar's
House. Early morning.
Enter* CAESAR *dressed.*

For 'Who's within?'
read 'Ho there!'

Horses did neigh, and dying men did groan,
And ghosts did shriek and squeal about the streets.
O Cæsar, these things are beyond all use,   25
And I do fear them !
CÆS.   What can be avoided,
Whose end is purpos'd by the mighty gods ?
Yet Cæsar shall go forth ; for these predictions
Are to the world in general as to Cæsar.
CAL. When beggars die there are no comets seen :   30
The heavens themselves blaze forth the death of princes.
CÆS. Cowards die many times before their deaths :
The valiant never taste of death but once.
Of all the wonders that I yet have heard,
It seems to me most strange that men should fear,   35
Seeing that death, a necessary end,
Will come when it will come.

Re-enter SERVANT.

                        What say the augurers ?
SERV. They would not have you to stir forth to-day.
Plucking the entrails of an offering forth,
They could not find a heart within the beast.   40
CÆS. The gods do this in shame of cowardice.
Cæsar should be a beast without a heart,
If he should stay at home to-day for fear.
No, Cæsar shall not.   Danger knows full well
That Cæsar is more dangerous than he :   45
We are two lions litter'd in one day,
And I the elder and more terrible ;
And Cæsar shall go forth.
CAL.   Alas, my lord,
Your wisdom is consum'd in confidence.
Do not go forth to-day.   Call it my fear   50
That keeps you in the house, and not your own.
We'll send Mark Antony to the Senate House,
And he shall say you are not well to-day.
Let me, upon my knee, prevail in this.
CÆS. Mark Antony shall say I am not well ;   55
And for thy humour I will stay at home.

Enter DECIUS.

Here's Decius Brutus, he shall tell them so.
DEC. Cæsar, all hail !   Good morrow, worthy Cæsar.
I come to fetch you to the Senate House.
CÆS. And you are come in very happy time,   60
To bear my greeting to the senators
And tell them that I will not come to-day.
Cannot, is false ; and that I dare not, falser ;
I will not come to-day.   Tell them so, Decius.
CAL. Say he is sick.
CÆS.   Shall Cæsar send a lie ?   65
Have I in conquest stretch'd mine arm so far,
To be afeard to tell greybeards the truth ?

Decius, go tell them Cæsar will not come.
DEC. Most mighty Cæsar, let me know some cause,
    Lest I be laugh'd at when I tell them so.   70
CÆS. The cause is in my will : I will not come.
    That is enough to satisfy the Senate.
    But for your private satisfaction,
    Because I love you, I will let you know :
    Calphurnia here, my wife, stays me at home.   75
    She dreamt to-night she saw my statua,
    Which, like a fountain with an hundred spouts,
    Did run pure blood ; and many lusty Romans
    Came smiling and did bathe their hands in it.
    And these does she apply for warnings and portents   80
    And evils imminent, and on her knee
    Hath begg'd that I will stay at home to-day.
DEC. This dream is all amiss interpreted ;
    It was a vision fair and fortunate.
    Your statue spouting blood in many pipes,   85
    In which so many smiling Romans bath'd,
    Signifies that from you great Rome shall suck
    Reviving blood, and that great men shall press
    For tinctures, stains, relics, and cognizance.
    This by Calphurnia's dream is signified.   90
CÆS. And this way have you well expounded it.
DEC. I have, when you have heard what I can say—
    And know it now : the Senate have concluded
    To give this day a crown to mighty Cæsar.
    If you shall send them word you will not come,   95
    Their minds may change.   Besides, it were a mock
    Apt to be render'd, for some one to say
    ' Break up the Senate till another time,
    When Cæsar's wife shall meet with better dreams'.
    If Cæsar hide himself, shall they not whisper   100
    ' Lo, Cæsar is afraid ' ?
    Pardon me, Cæsar ; for my dear dear love
    To your proceeding bids me tell you this,
    And reason to my love is liable.
CÆS. How foolish do your fears seem now, Calphurnia !   105
    I am ashamed I did yield to them.
    Give me my robe, for I will go.

Enter BRUTUS, LIGARIUS, METELLUS, CASCA, TREBONIUS, CINNA,
and PUBLIUS.

    And look where Publius is come to fetch me.
PUB. Good morrow, Cæsar.
CÆS.   Welcome, Publius.
    What, Brutus, are you stirr'd so early too ?   110
    Good morrow, Casca.   Caius Ligarius,
    Cæsar was ne'er so much your enemy
    As that same ague which hath made you lean.
    What is't o'clock ?
BRU.   Cæsar, 'tis strucken eight.
CÆS. I thank you for your pains and courtesy.   115

Enter ANTONY.

See ! Antony, that revels long o' nights,
Is notwithstanding up.   Good morrow, Antony.
ANT. So to most noble Cæsar.
CÆS.   Bid them prepare within.
I am to blame to be thus waited for.
Now, Cinna.   Now, Metellus.   What, Trebonius !   120
I have an hour's talk in store for you.
Remember that you call on me to-day ;
Be near me, that I may remember you.
TREB. Cæsar, I will. [*Aside*.]   And so near will I be,
That your best friends shall wish I had been further.   125
CÆS. Good friends, go in and taste some wine with me ;
And we, like friends, will straightway go together.
BRU. [*Aside*.]   That every like is not the same, O Cæsar,
The heart of Brutus yearns to think upon !   [*Exeunt*.

SCENE III.   *Rome. A street near the Capitol.*

Enter ARTEMIDORUS *reading a paper.*

ART. ' Cæsar, beware of Brutus ; take heed of Cassius ; come not
near Casca ; have an eye to Cinna ; trust not Trebonius ; mark
well Metellus Cimber ; Decius Brutus loves thee not ; thou hast
wrong'd Caius Ligarius.   There is but one mind in all these men,
and it is bent against Cæsar.   If thou beest not immortal, look
about you.   Security gives way to conspiracy.   The mighty gods
defend thee !   6

Thy lover,
ARTEMIDORUS.'

Here will I stand till Cæsar pass along,
And as a suitor will I give him this.
My heart laments that virtue cannot live   10
Out of the teeth of emulation.
If thou read this, O Cæsar, thou mayest live ;
If not, the fates with traitors do contrive.   [*Exit*.

SCENE IV.   *Rome.   Before the house of Brutus.*

Enter PORTIA *and* LUCIUS.

POR. I prithee, boy, run to the Senate House.
Stay not to answer me, but get thee gone.
Why dost thou stay ?
LUC.   To know my errand, madam.
POR. I would have had thee there and here again,
Ere I can tell thee what thou shouldst do there.   5
[*Aside*.]   O constancy, be strong upon my side !
Set a huge mountain 'tween my heart and tongue !
I have a man's mind, but a woman's might.
How hard it is for women to keep counsel !—
Art thou here yet ?
LUC.   Madam, what should I do ?   10
Run to the Capitol, and nothing else ?

SCENE 6
*Exterior. Rome.
A Street. Day.*

SCENE 7
*Exterior. The street
outside Brutus' House.
Day.*

And so return to you, and nothing else ?
POR. Yes, bring me word, boy, if thy lord look well,
    For he went sickly forth ; and take good note
    What Cæsar doth, what suitors press to him.   15
    Hark, boy ! What noise is that ?
LUC. I hear none, madam.
POR.   Prithee listen well.
    I heard a bustling rumour, like a fray,
    And the wind brings it from the Capitol.
LUC. Sooth, madam, I hear nothing.

                Enter the SOOTHSAYER.

POR.   Come hither, fellow.   20
    Which way hast thou been ?
SOOTH.   At mine own house, good lady.
POR. What is't o'clock ?
SOOTH.   About the ninth hour, lady.
POR. Is Cæsar yet gone to the Capitol ?
SOOTH. Madam, not yet.   I go to take my stand,
    To see him pass on to the Capitol.   25
POR. Thou hast some suit to Cæsar, hast thou not ?
SOOTH. That I have, lady.   If it will please Cæsar
    To be so good to Cæsar as to hear me,
    I shall beseech him to befriend himself.
POR. Why, know'st thou any harm's intended towards him ?   30
SOOTH. None that I know will be, much that I fear may chance.
    Good morrow to you.   Here the street is narrow ;
    The throng that follows Cæsar at the heels,
    Of senators, of prætors, common suitors,
    Will crowd a feeble man almost to death.   35
    I'll get me to a place more void, and there
    Speak to great Cæsar as he comes along.   [*Exit.*
POR. I must go in.   [*Aside.*]   Ay me, how weak a thing
    The heart of woman is !   O Brutus,
    The heavens speed thee in thine enterprise !   40
    Sure the boy heard me.—Brutus hath a suit
    That Cæsar will not grant.—O, I grow faint.—
    Run, Lucius, and commend me to my lord ;
    Say I am merry.   Come to me again,
    And bring me word what he doth say to thee.   45
                                    [*Exeunt severally.*

ACT THREE

SCENE I.   *Rome. A street before the Capitol.*

Flourish.   Enter CÆSAR, BRUTUS, CASSIUS, CASCA, DECIUS, METELLUS,
    TREBONIUS, CINNA, ANTONY, LEPIDUS, ARTEMIDORUS, POPILIUS,
    PUBLIUS, *and the* SOOTHSAYER.

CÆS. The ides of March are come.
SOOTH. Ay, Cæsar, but not gone.
ART. Hail, Cæsar! Read this schedule.
DEC. Trebonius doth desire you to o'er-read,
    At your best leisure, this his humble suit.   5

SCENE 8
Exterior. Rome.
A Street. Day.

ART. O Cæsar, read mine first ; for mine's a suit
    That touches Cæsar nearer.   Read it, great Cæsar.
CÆS. What touches us ourself shall be last serv'd.
ART. Delay not, Cæsar ; read it instantly.
CÆS. What, is the fellow mad ?
PUB.   Sirrah, give place.   10
CAS. What, urge you your petitions in the street ?
    Come to the Capitol.

       CÆSAR *enters the Capitol, the rest following.*

POP. I wish your enterprise to-day may thrive.
CAS. What enterprise, Popilius ?
POP.   Fare you well.   [*Advances to* CÆSAR.
BRU. What said Popilius Lena ?   15
CAS. He wish'd to-day our enterprise might thrive.
    I fear our purpose is discovered.
BRU. Look how he makes to Cæsar.   Mark him.
CAS. Casca, be sudden, for we fear prevention.
    Brutus, what shall be done ?   If this be known,   20
    Cassius or Cæsar never shall turn back,
    For I will slay myself.
BRU.   Cassius, be constant.
    Popilius Lena speaks not of our purposes ;
    For look, he smiles, and Cæsar doth not change.
CAS. Trebonius knows his time ; for look you, Brutus,   25
    He draws Mark Antony out of the way.
                 [*Exeunt* ANTONY *and* TREBONIUS.
DEC. Where is Metellus Cimber ?   Let him go
    And presently prefer his suit to Cæsar.
BRU. He is address'd ; press near and second him.
CIN. Casca, you are the first that rears your hand.   30
CÆS. Are we all ready ?   What is now amiss
    That Cæsar and his Senate must redress ?
MET. Most high, most mighty, and most puissant Cæsar,
    Metellus Cimber throws before thy seat
    An humble heart.   [*Kneeling.*
CÆS.   I must prevent thee, Cimber.   35
    These couchings and these lowly courtesies
    Might fire the blood of ordinary men,
    And turn pre-ordinance and first decree
    Into the law of children.   Be not fond
    To think that Cæsar bears such rebel blood   40
    That will be thaw'd from the true quality
    With that which melteth fools—I mean, sweet words,
    Low-crooked curtsies, and base spaniel fawning.
    Thy brother by decree is banished ;
    If thou dost bend, and pray, and fawn for him,   45
    I spurn thee like a cur out of my way.
    Know, Cæsar doth not wrong ; nor without cause
    Will he be satisfied.
MET. Is there no voice more worthy than my own
    To sound more sweetly in great Cæsar's ear   50
    For the repealing of my banish'd brother ?
BRU. I kiss thy hand, but not in flattery, Cæsar,

SCENE 9
*Exterior. Rome. Outside
the Senate House. Day.*
POPILIUS, CASCA,
BRUTUS

SCENE 10
*Interior. The Senate
House. Day.*
CAESAR, ANTONY,
BRUTUS, CASSIUS,
CASCA, DECIUS,
METELLUS, TREBONIUS,
CINNA, LEPIDUS,
POPILIUS, PUBLIUS

| 'Are we all ready?'
omitted.

Desiring thee that Publius Cimber may
Have an immediate freedom of repeal.
CÆS. What, Brutus !
CAS.   Pardon, Cæsar ! Cæsar, pardon !   55
As low as to thy foot doth Cassius fall,
To beg enfranchisement for Publius Cimber.
CÆS. I could be well mov'd, if I were as you ;
If I could pray to move, prayers would move me ;
But I am constant as the northern star,   60
Of whose true-fix'd and resting quality
There is no fellow in the firmament.
The skies are painted with unnumb'red sparks,
They are all fire, and every one doth shine ;
But there's but one in all doth hold his place.   65
So in the world : 'tis furnish'd well with men,
And men are flesh and blood, and apprehensive ;
Yet in the number I do know but one
That unassailable holds on his rank,
Unshak'd of motion ; and that I am he,   70
Let me a little show it, even in this—
That I was constant Cimber should be banish'd,
And constant do remain to keep him so.
CIN. O Cæsar !
CÆS.   Hence ! Wilt thou lift up Olympus ?
DEC. Great Cæsar !
CÆS.   Doth not Brutus bootless kneel ?   75
CASCA. Speak, hands, for me !   [*They stab* CÆSAR. CASCA
          strikes the first, BRUTUS *the last blow.*
CÆS. Et tu, Brute ?—Then fall, Cæsar !   [*Dies.*
CIN. Liberty ! Freedom ! Tyranny is dead !
Run hence, proclaim, cry it about the streets.
CAS. Some to the common pulpits, and cry out   80
' Liberty, freedom, and enfranchisement ! '
BRU. People and Senators, be not affrighted.
Fly not ; stand still. Ambition's debt is paid.
CASCA. Go to the pulpit, Brutus.
DEC. And Cassius too.   85
BRU. Where's Publius ?
CIN. Here, quite confounded with this mutiny.
MET. Stand fast together, lest some friend of Cæsar's
Should chance—
BRU. Talk not of standing. Publius, good cheer !   90
There is no harm intended to your person,
Nor to no Roman else. So tell them, Publius.
CAS. And leave us, Publius, lest that the people,
Rushing on us, should do your age some mischief.
BRU. Do so ; and let no man abide this deed   95
But we the doers.

Re-enter TREBONIUS.

CAS. Where is Antony ?
TREB.   Fled to his house amaz'd.
Men, wives, and children, stare, cry out, and run,
As it were doomsday.

BRU. Fates, we will know your pleasures.
That we shall die, we know ; 'tis but the time, 100
And drawing days out, that men stand upon.
CAS. Why, he that cuts off twenty years of life
Cuts off so many years of fearing death.
BRU. Grant that, and then is death a benefit.
So are we Cæsar's friends, that have abridg'd 105
His time of fearing death. Stoop, Romans, stoop,
And let us bathe our hands in Cæsar's blood
Up to the elbows, and besmear our swords.
Then walk we forth, even to the market-place,
And waving our red weapons o'er our heads, 110
Let's all cry ' Peace, freedom, and liberty ! '
CAS. Stoop then, and wash. How many ages hence
Shall this our lofty scene be acted over
In states unborn and accents yet unknown !
BRU. How many times shall Cæsar bleed in sport, 115
That now on Pompey's basis lies along
No worthier than the dust !
CAS. So oft as that shall be,
So often shall the knot of us be call'd
The men that gave their country liberty.
DEC. What, shall we forth ?
CAS. Ay, every man away. 120
Brutus shall lead, and we will grace his heels
With the most boldest and best hearts of Rome.

Enter a SERVANT.

BRU. Soft, who comes here ? A friend of Antony's.
SERV. Thus, Brutus, did my master bid me kneel ;
Thus did Mark Antony bid me fall down ; 125
And, being prostrate, thus he bade me say :
Brutus is noble, wise, valiant, and honest ;
Cæsar was mighty, bold, royal, and loving.
Say I love Brutus, and I honour him ;
Say I fear'd Cæsar, honour'd him, and lov'd him. 130
If Brutus will vouchsafe that Antony
May safely come to him, and be resolv'd
How Cæsar hath deserv'd to lie in death,
Mark Antony shall not love Cæsar dead
So well as Brutus living ; but will follow 135
The fortunes and affairs of noble Brutus
Through the hazards of this untrod state
With all true faith. So says my master Antony.
BRU. Thy master is a wise and valiant Roman ;
I never thought him worse. 140
Tell him, so please him come unto this place,
He shall be satisfied and, by my honour,
Depart untouch'd.
SERV. I'll fetch him presently. [*Exit.*
BRU. I know that we shall have him well to friend.
CAS. I wish we may. But yet have I a mind 145
That fears him much ; and my misgiving still
Falls shrewdly to the purpose.

Calphurnia (Elizabeth Spriggs), Julius Caesar (Charles Gray) and Mark Antony (Keith Michell)

Virginia McKenna as Portia with the Soothsayer (Ronald Forfar)

John Tordoff as Cinna the Poet

Keith Michell as Mark Antony

Keith Michell as Mark Antony and Garrick Hagon as Octavius Caesar

Richard Pasco as Marcus Brutus with (left to right) Dardanius (Michael Jenkinson), Strato (Maurice Thorogood) and Clitus (Christopher Good)

Marcus Brutus (Richard Pasco) and (behind, right) Messala (Brian Coburn) look down at the bodies of Cassius (David Collings) and Titinius (Leonard Preston)

Re-enter ANTONY.

| BRU. But here comes Antony. Welcome, Mark Antony.
ANT. O mighty Cæsar! dost thou lie so low ?
  Are all thy conquests, glories, triumphs, spoils, 150
  Shrunk to this little measure ? Fare thee well.
  I know not, gentlemen, what you intend,
  Who else must be let blood, who else is rank.
  If I myself, there is no hour so fit
  As Cæsar's death's hour ; nor no instrument 155
  Of half that worth as those your swords, made rich
  With the most noble blood of all this world.
  I do beseech ye, if you bear me hard,
  Now, whilst your purpled hands do reek and smoke,
  Fulfil your pleasure. Live a thousand years, 160
  I shall not find myself so apt to die.
  No place will please me so, no mean of death,
  As here by Cæsar, and by you cut off,
  The choice and master spirits of this age.
BRU. O Antony ! beg not your death of us. 165
  Though now we must appear bloody and cruel,
  As by our hands and this our present act
  You see we do ; yet see you but our hands,
  And this the bleeding business they have done.
  Our hearts you see not ; they are pitiful ; 170
  And pity to the general wrong of Rome,
  As fire drives out fire, so pity pity,
  Hath done this deed on Cæsar. For your part,
  To you our swords have leaden points, Mark Antony ;
  Our arms in strength of malice, and our hearts 175
  Of brothers' temper, do receive you in
  With all kind love, good thoughts, and reverence.
CAS. Your voice shall be as strong as any man's
  In the disposing of new dignities.
BRU. Only be patient till we have appeas'd 180
  The multitude, beside themselves with fear,
  And then we will deliver you the cause
  Why I, that did love Cæsar when I struck him,
  Have thus proceeded.
ANT.   I doubt not of your wisdom.
  Let each man render me his bloody hand. 185
  First, Marcus Brutus, will I shake with you ;
  Next, Caius Cassius, do I take your hand ;
  Now, Decius Brutus, yours ; now yours, Metellus ;
  Yours, Cinna ; and my valiant Casca, yours.
  Though last, not least in love, yours, good Trebonius. 190
  Gentlemen all—alas, what shall I say ?
  My credit now stands on such slippery ground
  That one of two bad ways you must conceit me,
  Either a coward or a flatterer.
  That I did love thee, Cæsar, O, 'tis true ! 195
  If then thy spirit look upon us now,
  Shall it not grieve thee dearer than thy death
  To see thy Antony making his peace,

| 'But here comes
Antony' omitted.

David Collings as Cassius, Sam Dastor as Casca and Richard Pasco as Brutus

Virginia McKenna as Portia and Richard Pasco as Brutus

Keith Michell as Mark Antony with the body of Julius Caesar (Charles Gray)

Shaking the bloody fingers of thy foes,
Most noble ! in the presence of thy corse ?   200
Had I as many eyes as thou hast wounds,
Weeping as fast as they stream forth thy blood,
It would become me better than to close
In terms of friendship with thine enemies.
Pardon me, Julius !   Here wast thou bay'd, brave hart ;   205
Here didst thou fall ;   and here thy hunters stand,
Sign'd in thy spoil, and crimson'd in thy Lethe.
O world, thou wast the forest to this hart ;
And this indeed, O world, the heart of thee !
How like a deer strucken by many princes   210
Dost thou here lie !
CAS. Mark Antony—
ANT.   Pardon me, Caius Cassius.
The enemies of Cæsar shall say this ;
Then, in a friend, it is cold modesty.
CAS. I blame you not for praising Cæsar so ;   215
But what compact mean you to have with us ?
Will you be prick'd in number of our friends,
Or shall we on, and not depend on you ?
ANT. Therefore I took your hands ; but was indeed
Sway'd from the point by looking down on Cæsar.   220
Friends am I with you all, and love you all,
Upon this hope, that you shall give me reasons
Why and wherein Cæsar was dangerous.
BRU. Or else were this a savage spectacle.
Our reasons are so full of good regard   225
That were you, Antony, the son of Cæsar,
You should be satisfied.
ANT.   That's all I seek ;
And am moreover suitor that I may
Produce his body to the market-place
And, in the pulpit, as becomes a friend,   230
Speak in the order of his funeral.
BRU. You shall, Mark Antony.
CAS.   Brutus, a word with you.
[Aside to BRUTUS.]   You know not what you do.   Do not consent
That Antony speak in his funeral.
Know you how much the people may be mov'd   235
By that which he will utter ?
BRU. [Aside to CASSIUS.]   By your pardon—
I will myself into the pulpit first,
And show the reason of our Cæsar's death.
What Antony shall speak, I will protest
He speaks by leave and by permission ;   240
And that we are contented Cæsar shall
Have all true rites and lawful ceremonies.
It shall advantage more than do us wrong.
CAS. I know not what may fall.   I like it not.
BRU. Mark Antony, here, take you Cæsar's body.   245
You shall not in your funeral speech blame us,
But speak all good you can devise of Cæsar ;
And say you do't by our permission ;

Else shall you not have any hand at all
About his funeral.   And you shall speak   250
In the same pulpit whereto I am going,
After my speech is ended.
ANT.   Be it so ;
I do desire no more.
BRU. Prepare the body then, and follow us.   [*Exeunt all but* ANTONY.
ANT. O, pardon me, thou bleeding piece of earth,   255
That I am meek and gentle with these butchers !
Thou art the ruins of the noblest man
That ever lived in the tide of times.
Woe to the hand that shed this costly blood !
Over thy wounds now do I prophesy—   260
Which like dumb mouths do ope their ruby lips
To beg the voice and utterance of my tongue—
A curse shall light upon the limbs of men ;
Domestic fury and fierce civil strife
Shall cumber all the parts of Italy ;   265
Blood and destruction shall be so in use,
And dreadful objects so familiar,
That mothers shall but smile when they behold
Their infants quartered with the hands of war,
All pity chok'd with custom of fell deeds ;   270
And Cæsar's spirit, ranging for revenge,
With Até by his side come hot from hell,
Shall in these confines with a monarch's voice
Cry ' Havoc ! ' and let slip the dogs of war,
That this foul deed shall smell above the earth   275
With carrion men, groaning for burial.

Enter Octavius' SERVANT.

You serve Octavius Cæsar, do you not ?
SERV. I do, Mark Antony.
ANT. Cæsar did write for him to come to Rome.
SERV. He did receive his letters, and is coming,   280
And bid me say to you by word of mouth—
O Cæsar !   [*Seeing the body.*
ANT. Thy heart is big, get thee apart and weep.
Passion, I see, is catching ; for mine eyes,
Seeing those beads of sorrow stand in thine,   285
Began to water.   Is thy master coming ?
SERV. He lies to-night within seven leagues of Rome.
ANT. Post back with speed, and tell him what hath chanc'd.
Here is a mourning Rome, a dangerous Rome,
No Rome of safety for Octavius yet ;   290
Hie hence and tell him so.   Yet stay awhile ;
Thou shalt not back till I have borne this corse
Into the market-place.   There shall I try,
In my oration, how the people take
The cruel issue of these bloody men ;   295
According to the which thou shalt discourse
To young Octavius of the state of things.
Lend me your hand.   [*Exeunt with Cæsar's body.* | Line 298 and
                                                              stage direction
                                                              omitted.

Scene II. *Rome. The Forum.*

Enter BRUTUS *and* CASSIUS, *with the* PLEBEIANS.

CITIZENS. We will be satisfied ! Let us be satisfied !
BRU. Then follow me, and give me audience, friends.
Cassius, go you into the other street,
And part the numbers.
Those that will hear me speak, let 'em stay here ;   5
Those that will follow Cassius, go with him ;
And public reasons shall be rendered
Of Cæsar's death.
1 PLEB.   I will hear Brutus speak.
2 PLEB. I will hear Cassius, and compare their reasons,
When severally we hear them rendered.   [*Exit* CASSIUS, *with
    some of the* PLEBEIANS. BRUTUS *goes into the pulpit.*
3 PLEB. The noble Brutus is ascended.   Silence !   11
BRU. Be patient till the last.
Romans, countrymen, and lovers ! hear me for my cause, and be
silent, that you may hear.   Believe me for mine honour, and have
respect to mine honour, that you may believe.   Censure me in
your wisdom, and awake your senses, that you may the better
judge.   If there be any in this assembly, any dear friend of
Cæsar's, to him I say that Brutus' love to Cæsar was no less
than his.   If then that friend demand why Brutus rose against
Cæsar, this is my answer : Not that I lov'd Cæsar less, but
that I lov'd Rome more.   Had you rather Cæsar were living,
and die all slaves, than that Cæsar were dead, to live all
free men ?   As Cæsar lov'd me, I weep for him ; as he was
fortunate, I rejoice at it ; as he was valiant, I honour him ; but—
as he was ambitious, I slew him.   There is tears for his love ;
joy for his fortune ; honour for his valour ; and death for his
ambition.   Who is here so base that would be a bondman ?
If any, speak ; for him have I offended.   Who is here so rude
that would not be a Roman ?   If any, speak ; for him have I
offended.   Who is here so vile that will not love his country ?   If
any, speak ; for him have I offended.   I pause for a reply.   33
ALL. None, Brutus, none.
BRU. Then none have I offended.   I have done no more to Cæsar
than you shall do to Brutus.   The question of his death is enroll'd
in the Capitol ; his glory not extenuated, wherein he was worthy ;
nor his offences enforc'd, for which he suffered death.   39

Enter MARK ANTONY *and* OTHERS *with Cæsar's body.*

Here comes his body, mourn'd by Mark Antony, who, though he
had no hand in his death, shall receive the benefit of his dying, a
place in the commonwealth, as which of you shall not ?   With this
I depart, that, as I slew my best lover for the good of Rome, I
have the same dagger for myself, when it shall please my country
to need my death.   46
ALL. Live, Brutus ! live, live !
1 PLEB. Bring him with triumph home unto his house.
2 PLEB. Give him a statue with his ancestors.

3 PLEB. Let him be Cæsar.
4 PLEB.   Cæsar's better parts   50
  Shall be crown'd in Brutus.
1 PLEB. We'll bring him to his house with shouts and clamours.
BRU. My countrymen—
2 PLEB.   Peace, silence ! Brutus speaks.
1 PLEB. Peace, ho !
BRU. Good countrymen, let me depart alone,   55
  And for my sake stay here with Antony.
  Do grace to Cæsar's corpse, and grace his speech
  Tending to Cæsar's glories, which Mark Antony
  By our permission, is allow'd to make.
  I do entreat you, not a man depart   60
  Save I alone, till Antony have spoke.   [Exit.
1 PLEB. Stay, ho ! and let us hear Mark Antony.
3 PLEB. Let him go up into the public chair.
  We'll hear him.   Noble Antony, go up.
ANT. For Brutus' sake I am beholding to you.   [Goes up.
4 PLEB. What does he say of Brutus ?
3 PLEB.   He says, for Brutus' sake
  He finds himself beholding to us all.
4 PLEB. 'Twere best he speak no harm of Brutus here.
1 PLEB. This Cæsar was a tyrant.
3 PLEB.   Nay, that's certain.
  We are blest that Rome is rid of him.   70
2 PLEB. Peace ! let us hear what Antony can say.
ANT. You gentle Romans—
ALL.   Peace, ho ! let us hear him.
ANT. Friends, Romans, countrymen, lend me your ears;
  I come to bury Cæsar, not to praise him.
  The evil that men do lives after them ;   75
  The good is oft interred with their bones ;
  So let it be with Cæsar.   The noble Brutus
  Hath told you Cæsar was ambitious.
  If it were so, it was a grievous fault ;
  And grievously hath Cæsar answer'd it.   80
  Here, under leave of Brutus and the rest—
  For Brutus is an honourable man ;
  So are they all, all honourable men—
  Come I to speak in Cæsar's funeral.
  He was my friend, faithful and just to me ;   85
  But Brutus says he was ambitious,
  And Brutus is an honourable man.
  He hath brought many captives home to Rome,
  Whose ransoms did the general coffers fill ;
  Did this in Cæsar seem ambitious ?   90
  When that the poor have cried, Cæsar hath wept ;
  Ambition should be made of sterner stuff.
  Yet Brutus says he was ambitious ;
  And Brutus is an honourable man.
  You all did see that on the Lupercal   95
  I thrice presented him a kingly crown,
  Which he did thrice refuse.   Was this ambition ?
  Yet Brutus says he was ambitious ;

And sure he is an honourable man.
I speak not to disprove what Brutus spoke,   100
But here I am to speak what I do know.
You all did love him once, not without cause ;
What cause witholds you, then, to mourn for him ?
O judgment, thou art fled to brutish beasts,
And men have lost their reason !   Bear with me ;   105
My heart is in the coffin there with Cæsar,
And I must pause till it come back to me.
1 PLEB. Methinks there is much reason in his sayings.
2 PLEB. If thou consider rightly of the matter,
Cæsar has had great wrong.
3 PLEB.   Has he, masters !   110
I fear there will a worse come in his place.
4 PLEB. Mark'd ye his words ?   He would not take the crown ;
Therefore 'tis certain he was not ambitious.
1 PLEB. If it be found so, some will dear abide it.
2 PLEB. Poor soul ! his eyes are red as fire with weeping. 115
3 PLEB. There's not a nobler man in Rome than Antony.
4 PLEB. Now mark him, he begins again to speak.
ANT. But yesterday the word of Cæsar might
Have stood against the world : now lies he there,
And none so poor to do him reverence.   120
O masters, if I were dispos'd to stir
Your hearts and minds to mutiny and rage,
I should do Brutus wrong, and Cassius wrong,
Who, you all know, are honourable men.
I will not do them wrong ; I rather choose   125
To wrong the dead, to wrong myself and you,
Than I will wrong such honourable men.
But here's a parchment with the seal of Cæsar
I found it in his closet—'tis his will.
Let but the commons hear this testament,   130
Which, pardon me, I do not mean to read,
And they would go and kiss dead Cæsar's wounds
And dip their napkins in his sacred blood ;
Yea, beg a hair of him for memory
And, dying, mention it within their wills,   135
Bequeathing it as a rich legacy
Unto their issue.
4 PLEB. We'll hear the will.   Read it, Mark Antony.
ALL. The will, the will !   We will hear Cæsar's will.
ANT. Have patience, gentle friends, I must not read it ; 140
It is not meet you know how Cæsar lov'd you.
You are not wood, you are not stones, but men ;
And being men, hearing the will of Cæsar,
It will inflame you, it will make you mad.
'Tis good you know not that you are his heirs ;   145
For if you should, O, what would come of it ?
4 PLEB. Read the will ; we'll hear it, Antony !
You shall read us the will—Cæsar's will.
ANT. Will you be patient ?   Will you stay awhile ?
I have o'ershot myself to tell you of it.   150
I fear I wrong the honourable men

Whose daggers have stabb'd Cæsar ; I do fear it.
4 PLEB. They were traitors. Honourable men !
ALL. The will ! the testament !   154
2 PLEB. They were villains, murderers. The will ! Read the will.
ANT. You will compel me, then, to read the will ?
   Then make a ring about the corpse of Cæsar,
   And let me show you him that made the will.
   Shall I descend ? and will you give me leave ?   160
ALL. Come down.
2 PLEB. Descend.   [ANTONY comes down.
3 PLEB. You shall have leave.
4 PLEB. A ring ! Stand round.
1 PLEB. Stand from the hearse, stand from the body.   165
2 PLEB. Room for Antony, most noble Antony !
ANT. Nay, press not so upon me ; stand far off.
ALL. Stand back. Room ! Bear back.
ANT. If you have tears, prepare to shed them now.
   You all do know this mantle. I remember   170
   The first time ever Cæsar put it on ;
   'Twas on a summer's evening, in his tent,
   That day he overcame the Nervii.
   Look ! in this place ran Cassius' dagger through ;
   See what a rent the envious Casca made ;   175
   Through this the well-beloved Brutus stabb'd,
   And as he pluck'd his cursed steel away,
   Mark how the blood of Cæsar follow'd it,
   As rushing out of doors, to be resolv'd
   If Brutus so unkindly knock'd or no ;   180
   For Brutus, as you know, was Cæsar's angel.
   Judge, O you gods, how dearly Cæsar lov'd him !
   This was the most unkindest cut of all ;
   For when the noble Cæsar saw him stab,
   Ingratitude, more strong than traitors' arms,   185
   Quite vanquish'd him. Then burst his mighty heart ;
   And in his mantle muffling up his face,
   Even at the base of Pompey's statua,
   Which all the while ran blood, great Cæsar fell.
   O, what a fall was there, my countrymen !   190
   Then I, and you, and all of us fell down,
   Whilst bloody treason flourish'd over us.
   O, now you weep, and I perceive you feel
   The dint of pity. These are gracious drops.
   Kind souls, what weep you when you but behold   195
   Our Cæsar's vesture wounded ? Look you here,
   Here is himself, marr'd as you see with traitors.
1 PLEB. O piteous spectacle !
2 PLEB. O noble Cæsar !
3 PLEB. O woeful day !   200
4 PLEB. O traitors, villains !
1 PLEB. O most bloody sight !
2 PLEB. We will be reveng'd.
ALL. Revenge ! About ! Seek ! Burn ! Fire ! Kill ! Slay ! Let
   not a traitor live !   205
ANT. Stay, countrymen.

1 PLEB. Peace there! Hear the noble Antony.
2 PLEB. We'll hear him, we'll follow him, we'll die with him.
ANT. Good friends, sweet friends, let me not stir you up   210
　　To such a sudden flood of mutiny.
　　They that have done this deed are honourable.
　　What private griefs they have, alas, I know not,
　　That made them do it; they are wise and honourable,
　　And will, no doubt, with reasons answer you.   215
　　I come not, friends, to steal away your hearts;
　　I am no orator, as Brutus is,
　　But, as you know me all, a plain blunt man,
　　That love my friend; and that they know full well
　　That gave me public leave to speak of him.   220
　　For I have neither wit, nor words, nor worth,
　　Action, nor utterance, nor the power of speech,
　　To stir men's blood; I only speak right on.
　　I tell you that which you yourselves do know;
　　Show you sweet Cæsar's wounds, poor poor dumb mouths,   225
　　And bid them speak for me.　But were I Brutus,
　　And Brutus Antony, there were an Antony
　　Would ruffle up your spirits, and put a tongue
　　In every wound of Cæsar, that should move
　　The stones of Rome to rise and mutiny.   230
ALL. We'll mutiny.
1 PLEB. We'll burn the house of Brutus.
3 PLEB. Away, then! Come seek the conspirators.
ANT. Yet hear me, countrymen; yet hear me speak.
ALL. Peace, ho! Hear Antony, most noble Antony.   235
ANT. Why, friends, you go to do you know not what.
　　Wherein hath Cæsar thus deserv'd your loves?
　　Alas, you know not! I must tell you, then:
　　You have forgot the will I told you of.
ALL. Most true.　The will! Let's stay and hear the will.   240
ANT. Here is the will, and under Cæsar's seal:
　　To every Roman citizen he gives,
　　To every several man, seventy-five drachmas.
2 PLEB. Most noble Cæsar! We'll revenge his death.
3 PLEB. O royal Cæsar!   245
ANT. Hear me with patience.
ALL. Peace, ho!
ANT. Moreover, he hath left you all his walks,
　　His private arbours, and new-planted orchards,
　　On this side Tiber; he hath left them you,   250
　　And to your heirs for ever—common pleasures,
　　To walk abroad and recreate yourselves.
　　Here was a Cæsar! When comes such another?
1 PLEB. Never, never! Come away, away!
　　We'll burn his body in the holy place,   255
　　And with the brands fire the traitors' houses.
　　Take up the body.
2 PLEB. Go, fetch fire.
3 PLEB. Pluck down benches.
4 PLEB. Pluck down forms, windows, any thing.   260
　　　　　　　　[Exeunt PLEBEIANS with the body.

ANT. Now let it work.   Mischief, thou art afoot,
Take thou what course thou wilt.

Enter a SERVANT.

How now, fellow !
SERV. Sir, Octavius is already come to Rome.
ANT. Where is he ?
SERV. He and Lepidus are at Cæsar's house.   265
ANT. And thither will I straight to visit him.
He comes upon a wish.   Fortune is merry,
And in this mood will give us any thing.
SERV. I heard him say Brutus and Cassius
Are rid like madmen through the gates of Rome.   270
ANT. Belike they had some notice of the people,
How I had mov'd them.   Bring me to Octavius.   [*Exeunt.*

SCENE III. *Rome. A street.*

Enter CINNA *the* POET, *and after him the* PLEBEIANS.

CIN. I dreamt to-night that I did feast with Cæsar,
And things unluckily charge my fantasy.
I have no will to wander forth of doors,
Yet something leads me forth.
1 PLEB. What is your name ?   5
2 PLEB. Whither are you going ?
3 PLEB. Where do you dwell ?
4 PLEB. Are you a married man or a bachelor ?
2 PLEB. Answer every man directly.
1 PLEB. Ay, and briefly.   10
4 PLEB. Ay, and wisely.
3 PLEB. Ay, and truly, you were best.
CIN. What is my name ?   Whither am I going ?   Where do I dwell ?
Am I a married man or a bachelor ?   Then to answer every man
directly and briefly, wisely and truly : wisely, I say I am a
bachelor.   16
2 PLEB. That's as much as to say they are fools that marry.   You'll
bear me a bang for that, I fear.   Proceed directly.
CIN. Directly, I am going to Cæsar's funeral.   20
1 PLEB. As a friend or an enemy ?
CIN. As a friend.
2 PLEB. That matter is answered directly.
4 PLEB. For your dwelling—briefly.
CIN. Briefly, I dwell by the Capitol.   25
3 PLEB. Your name, sir, truly.
CIN. Truly, my name is Cinna.
1 PLEB. Tear him to pieces ; he's a conspirator !
CIN. I am Cinna the poet, I am Cinna the poet.
4 PLEB. Tear him for his bad verses, tear him for his bad verses !
CIN. I am not Cinna the conspirator.   32
4 PLEB. It is no matter, his name's Cinna ; pluck but his name out
of his heart, and turn him going.
3 PLEB. Tear him, tear him ! Come, brands, ho ! fire-brands !

SCENE 12
Exterior. Rome.
A Street. Night.

To Brutus', to Cassius'! Burn all! Some to Decius' house,
and some to Casca's ; some to Ligarius'.   Away, go !
[*Exeunt all the* PLEBEIANS *with* CINNA.

ACT FOUR

SCENE I. *Rome. Antony's house.*

Enter ANTONY, OCTAVIUS, *and* LEPIDUS.

	SCENE 13
	Interior. Antony's
	House. Day.

ANT. These many, then, shall die ; their names are prick'd.
OCT. Your brother too must die.   Consent you, Lepidus ?
LEP. I do consent.
OCT.   Prick him down, Antony.
LEP. Upon condition Publius shall not live,
 Who is your sister's son, Mark Antony.   5
ANT. He shall not live ; look, with a spot I damn him.
 But, Lepidus, go you to Cæsar's house ;
 Fetch the will hither, and we shall determine
 How to cut off some charge in legacies.
LEP. What, shall I find you here ?   10
OCT. Or here or at the Capitol.   [*Exit* LEPIDUS.
ANT. This is a slight unmeritable man,
 Meet to be sent on errands.   Is it fit,
 The threefold world divided, he should stand
 One of the three to share it ?
OCT.   So you thought him,   15
 And took his voice who should be prick'd to die
 In our black sentence and proscription.
ANT. Octavius, I have seen more days than you ;
 And though we lay these honours on this man,
 To ease ourselves of divers sland'rous loads,   20
 He shall but bear them as the ass bears gold,
 To groan and sweat under the business,
 Either led or driven as we point the way;
 And having brought our treasure where we will,
 Then take we down his load, and turn him off,   25
 Like to the empty ass, to shake his ears
 And graze in commons.
OCT.   You may do your will ;
 But he's a tried and valiant soldier.
ANT. So is my horse, Octavius, and for that
 I do appoint him store of provender.   30
 It is a creature that I teach to fight,
 To wind, to stop, to run directly on,
 His corporal motion govern'd by my spirit.
 And, in some taste, is Lepidus but so :
 He must be taught, and train'd, and bid go forth   35
 A barren-spirited fellow ; one that feeds
 On abjects, orts, and imitations,
 Which, out of use and stal'd by other men,
 Begin his fashion.   Do not talk of him
 But as a property.   And now, Octavius,   40

67

Listen great things : Brutus and Cassius
Are levying powers ; we must straight make head ;
Therefore let our alliance be combin'd,
Our best friends made, our means stretch'd ;
And let us presently go sit in council   45
How covert matters may be best disclos'd,
And open perils surest answered.
OCT. Let us do so ; for we are at the stake,
And bay'd about with many enemies ;
And some that smile have in their hearts, I fear,   50
Millions of mischiefs.   [*Exeunt.*

SCENE II.   *The Camp near Sardis.   Before the tent of Brutus.*

Drum.   Enter BRUTUS, LUCILIUS, LUCIUS, *and the* ARMY.
TITINIUS *and* PINDARUS *meet them.*

| BRU. Stand, ho !
| LUCIL. Give the word, ho ! and stand.
BRU. What now, Lucilius ?   Is Cassius near ?
LUCIL. He is at hand, and Pindarus is come
To do you salutation from his master.   5
BRU. He greets me well.   Your master, Pindarus,
In his own change, or by ill officers,
Hath given me some worthy cause to wish
Things done undone ; but if he be at hand
I shall be satisfied.
PIN.   I do not doubt   10
But that my noble master will appear
Such as he is, full of regard and honour.
BRU. He is not doubted.   A word, Lucilius,
How he receiv'd you ; let me be resolv'd.
LUCIL. With courtesy and with respect enough,   15
But not with such familiar instances
Nor with such free and friendly conference
As he hath us'd of old.
BRU.   Thou hast describ'd
A hot friend cooling.   Ever note, Lucilius,
When love begins to sicken and decay,   20
It useth an enforced ceremony.
There are no tricks in plain and simple faith ;
But hollow men, like horses hot at hand,
Make gallant show and promise of their mettle ;
But when they should endure the bloody spur,   25
They fall their crests, and like deceitful jades
Sink in the trial.   Comes his army on ?
LUCIL. They mean this night in Sardis to be quarter'd.
The greater part, the horse in general,
Are come with Cassius.   [*Low march within.*
| BRU.   Hark ! he is arriv'd :   30
March gently on to meet him.

Enter CASSIUS *and his* POWERS.

| CAS. Stand, ho !

SCENE 14
*Exterior. Sardis. Before
Brutus' Tent. Night.*

| Lines 1–2 omitted.

Stage direction and
'Hark!' omitted.

| 'Stand, ho!' omitted.

68

BRU. Stand, ho ! Speak the word along.
1 SOLD. Stand !
2 SOLD. Stand !   35
3 SOLD. Stand !
CAS. Most noble brother, you have done me wrong.
BRU. Judge me, you gods ! wrong I mine enemies ?
    And, if not so, how should I wrong a brother ?
CAS. Brutus, this sober form of yours hides wrongs ;   40
    And when you do them—
BRU.   Cassius, be content ;
    Speak your griefs softly ; I do know you well.
    Before the eyes of both our armies here,
    Which should perceive nothing but love from us,
    Let us not wrangle. Bid them move away ;   45
    Then in my tent, Cassius, enlarge your griefs,
    And I will give you audience.
CAS.   Pindarus,
    Bid our commanders lead their charges off
    A little from this ground.
BRU. Lucilius, do you the like ; and let no man   50
    Come to our tent till we have done our conference.
    Let Lucius and Titinius guard our door.   [*Exeunt.*

SCENE III. *The Camp near Sardis. Within the tent of Brutus.*

Enter BRUTUS *and* CASSIUS.

CAS. That you have wrong'd me doth appear in this :
    You have condemn'd and noted Lucius Pella
    For taking bribes here of the Sardians ;
    Wherein my letters, praying on his side,
    Because I knew the man, were slighted off.   5
BRU. You wrong'd yourself to write in such a case.
CAS. In such a time as this it is not meet
    That every nice offence should bear his comment.
BRU. Let me tell you, Cassius, you yourself
    Are much condemn'd to have an itching palm,   10
    To sell and mart your offices for gold
    To undeservers.
CAS.   I an itching palm !
    You know that you are Brutus that speaks this,
    Or, by the gods, this speech were else your last.
BRU. The name of Cassius honours this corruption,   15
    And chastisement doth therefore hide his head.
CAS. Chastisement !
BRU. Remember March, the ides of March remember :
    Did not great Julius bleed for justice' sake ?
    What villain touch'd his body, that did stab,
    And not for justice ? What, shall one of us,   20
    That struck the foremost man of all this world
    But for supporting robbers, shall we now
    Contaminate our fingers with base bribes,
    And sell the mighty space of our large honours
    For so much trash as may be grasped thus ?   25

Lines 34–36, for
'Stand!' read
'Stand, ho!'

SCENE 15
*Interior. Sardis.
Brutus' Tent. Night.*

69

I had rather be a dog and bay the moon
Than such a Roman.
CAS.   Brutus, bait not me !
I'll not endure it. You forget yourself,
To hedge me in. I am a soldier, I,   30
Older in practice, abler than yourself
To make conditions.
BRU.   Go to ; you are not, Cassius.
CAS. I am.
BRU. I say you are not.
CAS. Urge me no more, I shall forget myself ;   35
Have mind upon your health, tempt me no farther.
BRU. Away, slight man !
CAS. Is't possible ?
BRU.   Hear me, for I will speak.
Must I give way and room to your rash choler ?
Shall I be frighted when a madman stares ?   40
CAS. O ye gods, ye gods ! must I endure all this ?
BRU. All this ? Ay, more ! Fret till your proud heart break.
Go show your slaves how choleric you are,
And make your bondmen tremble. Must I budge ?
Must I observe you ? Must I stand and crouch   45
Under your testy humour ? By the gods,
You shall digest the venom of your spleen
Though it do split you ; for from this day forth
I'll use you for my mirth, yea, for my laughter,
When you are waspish.
CAS.   Is it come to this ?   50
BRU. You say you are a better soldier.
Let it appear so ; make your vaunting true,
And it shall please me well. For mine own part,
I shall be glad to learn of noble men.
CAS. You wrong me every way ; you wrong me, Brutus ;   55
I said an elder soldier, not a better.
Did I say ' better ' ?
BRU.   If you did, I care not.
CAS. When Cæsar liv'd, he durst not thus have mov'd me.
BRU. Peace, peace ! You durst not so have tempted him.
CAS. I durst not ?   60
BRU. No.
CAS. What, durst not tempt him ?
BRU.   For your life you durst not.
CAS. Do not presume too much upon my love ;
I may do that I shall be sorry for.
BRU. You have done that you should be sorry for.   65
There is no terror, Cassius, in your threats ;
For I am arm'd so strong in honesty
That they pass by me as the idle wind,
Which I respect not. I did send to you
For certain sums of gold, which you denied me ;   70
For I can raise no money by vile means.
By heaven, I had rather coin my heart,
And drop my blood for drachmas, than to wring
From the hard hands of peasants their vile trash

By any indirection. I did send   75
  To you for gold to pay my legions,
  Which you denied me ; was that done like Cassius ?
  Should I have answer'd Caius Cassius so ?
  When Marcus Brutus grows so covetous,
  To lock such rascal counters from his friends,   80
  Be ready, gods, with all your thunderbolts,
  Dash him to pieces !
CAS.   I denied you not.
BRU. You did.
CAS.   I did not. He was but a fool
  That brought my answer back.
  Brutus hath riv'd my heart.
  A friend should bear his friend's infirmities,   85
  But Brutus makes mine greater than they are.
BRU. I do not, till you practise them on me.
CAS. You love me not.
BRU.   I do not like your faults.
CAS. A friendly eye could never see such faults.
BRU. A flatterer's would not, though they do appear   90
  As huge as high Olympus.
CAS. Come, Antony, and young Octavius, come,
  Revenge yourselves alone on Cassius,
  For Cassius is aweary of the world :
  Hated by one he loves ; brav'd by his brother ;   95
  Check'd like a bondman ; all his faults observ'd,
  Set in a notebook, learn'd, and conn'd by rote,
  To cast into my teeth. O, I could weep
  My spirit from mine eyes ! There is my dagger,
  And here my naked breast ; within, a heart   100
  Dearer than Plutus' mine, richer than gold ;
  If that thou be'st a Roman, take it forth.
  I, that denied thee gold, will give my heart.
  Strike as thou didst at Cæsar ; for I know,
  When thou didst hate him worst, thou lov'dst him better   105
  Than ever thou lov'dst Cassius.
BRU.   Sheathe your dagger.
  Be angry when you will, it shall have scope ;
  Do what you will, dishonour shall be humour.
  O Cassius, you are yoked with a lamb,
  That carries anger as the flint bears fire ;   110
  Who, much enforced, shows a hasty spark,
  And straight is cold again.
CAS.   Hath Cassius liv'd
  To be but mirth and laughter to his Brutus,
  When grief and blood ill-temper'd vexeth him ?
BRU. When I spoke that I was ill-temper'd too.   115
CAS Do you confess so much ? Give me your hand.
BRU. And my heart too.
CAS.   O Brutus !
BRU.   What's the matter ?
CAS. Have not you love enough to bear with me,
  When that rash humour which my mother gave me
  Makes me forgetful ?

BRU. Yes, Cassius ; and from henceforth,   120
    When you are over-earnest with your Brutus,
    He'll think your mother chides, and leave you so.

Enter a POET, *followed by* LUCILIUS, TITINIUS, *and* LUCIUS.

POET. Let me go in to see the generals.
    There is some grudge between 'em ; 'tis not meet
    They be alone.
LUCIL. You shall not come to them.   125
POET. Nothing but death shall stay me.
CAS. How now ! What's the matter ?
POET. For shame, you generals ! What do you mean ?
    Love, and be friends, as two such men should be ;
    For I have seen more years, I'm sure, than ye.   130
CAS. Ha, ha ! How vilely doth this cynic rhyme !
BRU. Get you hence, sirrah ; saucy fellow, hence !
CAS. Bear with him, Brutus : 'tis his fashion.
BRU. I'll know his humour when he knows his time.
    What should the wars do with these jigging fools ?   135
    Companion, hence !
CAS.   Away, away, be gone !   [*Exit* POET.
BRU. Lucilius and Titinius, bid the commanders
    Prepare to lodge their companies to-night.
CAS. And come yourselves, and bring Messala with you
    Immediately to us.   [*Exeunt* LUCILIUS *and* TITINIUS.
BRU.   Lucius, a bowl of wine !   [*Exit* LUCIUS.
CAS. I did not think you could have been so angry.
BRU. O Cassius, I am sick of many griefs !
CAS. Of your philosophy you make no use,
    If you give place to accidental evils.
BRU. No man bears sorrow better. Portia is dead.   145
CAS. Ha ! Portia ?
BRU. She is dead.
CAS. How scap'd I killing when I cross'd you so ?
    O insupportable and touching loss !
    Upon what sickness ?
BRU.   Impatient of my absence,   150
    And grief that young Octavius with Mark Antony
    Have made themselves so strong ; for with her death
    That tidings came. With this she fell distract,
    And, her attendants absent, swallow'd fire.
CAS. And died so ?
BRU. Even so.
CAS. O ye immortal gods !   155

Enter LUCIUS *with wine and tapers.*

BRU. Speak no more of her. Give me a bowl of wine.
    In this I bury all unkindness, Cassius.   [*Drinks.*
CAS. My heart is thirsty for that noble pledge.
    Fill, Lucius, till the wine o'erswell the cup ;
    I cannot drink too much of Brutus' love. [*Drinks. Exit* LUCIUS

Re-enter TITINIUS, *with* MESSALA.

BRU. Gome in, Titinius ! Welcome, good Messala !

Now sit we close about this taper here,
And call in question our necessities.
CAS. Portia, art thou gone ?
BRU.   No more, I pray you.
Messala, I have here received letters,   165
That young Octavius and Mark Antony
Come down upon us with a mighty power,
Bending their expedition toward Philippi.
MES. Myself have letters of the self-same tenour.
BRU. With what addition ?   170
MES. That, by proscription and bills of outlawry,
Octavius, Antony, and Lepidus,
Have put to death an hundred senators.
BRU. Therein our letters do not well agree ;
Mine speak of seventy senators that died   175
By their proscriptions, Cicero being one.
CAS. Cicero one !
MES.   Cicero is dead,
And by that order of proscription.
Had you your letters from your wife, my lord ?
BRU. No, Messala.   180
MES. Nor nothing in your letters writ of her ?
BRU. Nothing, Messala.
MES.   That, methinks, is strange.
BRU. Why ask you ?   Hear you aught of her in yours ?
MES. No, my lord.
BRU. Now, as you are a Roman, tell me true.   185
MES. Then like a Roman bear the truth I tell :
For certain she is dead, and by strange manner.
BRU. Why, farewell, Portia.   We must die, Messala.
With meditating that she must die once,
I have the patience to endure it now.   190
MES. Even so great men great losses should endure.
CAS. I have as much of this in art as you,
But yet my nature could not bear it so.
BRU. Well, to our work alive.   What do you think
Of marching to Philippi presently ?   195
CAS. I do not think it good.
BRU.   Your reason ?
CAS.   This it is :
'Tis better that the enemy seek us ;
So shall he waste his means, weary his soldiers,
Doing himself offence, whilst we, lying still,
Are full of rest, defence, and nimbleness.   200
BRU. Good reasons must, of force, give place to better.
The people 'twixt Philippi and this ground
Do stand but in a forc'd affection ;
For they have grudg'd us contribution.
The enemy, marching along by them,   205
By them shall make a fuller number up,
Come on refresh'd, new-added, and encourag'd ;
From which advantage shall we cut him off,
If at Philippi we do face him there,
These people at our back.

CAS.	Hear me, good brother.	210

BRU. Under your pardon. You must note beside
That we have tried the utmost of our friends,
Our legions are brim full, our cause is ripe.
The enemy increaseth every day :
We, at the height, are ready to decline. 215
There is a tide in the affairs of men
Which, taken at the flood, leads on to fortune ;
Omitted, all the voyage of their life
Is bound in shallows and in miseries.
On such a full sea are we now afloat, 220
And we must take the current when it serves,
Or lose our ventures.
CAS.   Then, with your will, go on ;
We'll along ourselves and meet them at Philippi.
BRU. The deep of night is crept upon our talk,
And nature must obey necessity, 225
Which we will niggard with a little rest.
There is no more to say ?
CAS.   No more. Good night :
Early to-morrow will we rise, and hence.
| BRU. Lucius ! [*Enter* LUCIUS.] My gown. [*Exit* LUCIUS.] Farewell, | 'Lucius', 'My
good Messala. | gown' and
Good night, Titinius. Noble, noble Cassius, 230 | stage directions
Good night, and good repose ! | omitted.
CAS.   O my dear brother,
This was an ill beginning of the night !
Never come such division 'tween our souls !
Let it not, Brutus.
BRU.   Everything is well.
CAS. Good night, my lord.
BRU.   Good night, good brother. 235
TIT. *and* MES. Good night, Lord Brutus. | 'Good night . . . every
| BRU.   Farewell, every one. | one' omitted.
          [*Exeunt* CASSIUS, TITINIUS, *and* MESSALA.

          Re-enter LUCIUS *with the gown.*

Give me the gown. Where is thy instrument ?
LUC. Here in the tent.
BRU.   What, thou speak'st drowsily ?
Poor knave, I blame thee not ; thou art o'erwatched.
Call Claudius and some other of my men ; 240
I'll have them sleep on cushions in my tent.
LUC. Varro and Claudius !

          Enter VARRO *and* CLAUDIUS.

VAR. Calls my lord ?
BRU. I pray you, sirs, lie in my tent and sleep ;
It may be I shall raise you by and by 245
On business to my brother Cassius.
VAR. So please you we will stand and watch your pleasure.
BRU. I will not have it so. Lie down, good sirs ;
It may be I shall otherwise bethink me.
Look, Lucius, here's the book I sought for so ; 250

I put it in the pocket of my gown.
                    [VARRO *and* CLAUDIUS *lie down.*
LUC. I was sure your lordship did not give it me.
BRU. Bear with me, good boy, I am much forgetful.
Canst thou hold up thy heavy eyes awhile,
And touch thy instrument a strain or two ?   255
LUC. Ay, my lord, an't please you.
BRU.   It does, my boy.
I trouble thee too much, but thou art willing.
LUC. It is my duty, sir.
BRU. I should not urge thy duty past thy might ;
I know young bloods look for a time of rest.   260
LUC. I have slept, my lord, already.
BRU. It was well done ; and thou shalt sleep again ;
I will not hold thee long.   If I do live,
I will be good to thee. [*Music and a song.* LUCIUS *falls asleep.*
This is a sleepy tune.   O murd'rous slumber !   265
Layest thou thy leaden mace upon my boy,
That plays thee music ?   Gentle knave, good night.
I will not do thee so much wrong to wake thee.
If thou dost nod, thou break'st thy instrument ;
I'll take it from thee : and, good boy, good night.   270
Let me see, let me see ; is not the leaf turn'd down
Where I left reading ?   Here it is, I think.   [*Sits down.*

            Enter the GHOST *of* CÆSAR.

How ill this taper burns !   Ha !   who comes here ?
I think it is the weakness of mine eyes
That shapes this monstrous apparition.   275
It comes upon me.   Art thou any thing ?
Art thou some god, some angel, or some devil,
That mak'st my blood cold and my hair to stare ?
Speak to me what thou art.
GHOST. Thy evil spirit, Brutus.
BRU.   Why com'st thou ?   280
GHOST. To tell thee thou shalt see me at Philippi.
BRU. Well ; then I shall see thee again ?
GHOST. Ay, at Philippi.
BRU. Why, I will see thee at Philippi, then. [*Exit* Ghost.
Now I have taken heart thou vanishest.   285
Ill spirit, I would hold more talk with thee.
Boy ! Lucius ! Varro ! Claudius ! Sirs, awake !
Claudius !
LUC. The strings, my lord, are false.
BRU. He thinks he still is at his instrument.   290
Lucius, awake !
LUC. My lord !
BRU. Didst thou dream, Lucius, that thou so criedst out ?
LUC. My lord, I do not know that I did cry.
BRU. Yes, that thou didst.   Didst thou see any thing ?   295
LUC. Nothing, my lord.
BRU. Sleep again, Lucius.   Sirrah Claudius !
    [*To* VARRO.]   Fellow thou, awake !
VAR. My lord ?

CLAU. My lord ?   300
BRU. Why did you so cry out, sirs, in your sleep ?
BOTH. Did we, my lord ?
BRU.   Ay.   Saw you any thing ?
VAR. No, my lord, I saw nothing.
CLAU.   Nor I, my lord.
BRU. Go and commend me to my brother Cassius ;
    Bid him set on his pow'rs betimes before,   305
    And we will follow.
VAR. *and* CLAU. It shall be done, my lord.   [*Exeunt.*

ACT FIVE

SCENE I. *Near Philippi.*

Enter OCTAVIUS, ANTONY, *and their* ARMY.

SCENE 16
*Exterior. Near Philippi.
Day.*

OCT. Now, Antony, our hopes are answered.
    You said the enemy would not come down,
    But keep the hills and upper regions ;
    It proves not so.   Their battles are at hand ;
    They mean to warn us at Philippi here,   5
    Answering before we do demand of them.
ANT. Tut, I am in their bosoms, and I know
    Wherefore they do it.   They could be content
    To visit other places, and come down
    With fearful bravery, thinking by this face   10
    To fasten in our thoughts that they have courage ;
    But 'tis not so.

Enter a MESSENGER.

MESS.   Prepare you, generals :
    The enemy comes on in gallant show ;
    Their bloody sign of battle is hung out,
    And something to be done immediately.   15
ANT. Octavius, lead your battle softly on,
    Upon the left hand of the even field.
OCT. Upon the right hand I :   keep thou the left.
ANT. Why do you cross me in this exigent ?
OCT. I do not cross you ;   but I will do so.   [*March.*

Drum.   Enter BRUTUS, CASSIUS, *and their* ARMY ;   LUCILIUS,
TITINIUS, MESSALA, *and* OTHERS.

SCENE 17
*Exterior. Near Philippi.
Day.*
BRUTUS *and* CASSIUS
confront ANTONY *and*
OCTAVIUS

BRU. They stand, and would have parley.
CAS. Stand fast, Titinius ; we must out and talk.
OCT. Mark Antony, shall we give sign of battle ?
ANT. No, Cæsar, we will answer on their charge.
    Make forth ;   the generals would have some words.   25
OCT. Stir not until the signal.
BRU. Words before blows.   Is it so, countrymen ?
OCT. Not that we love words better, as you do.
BRU. Good words are better than bad strokes, Octavius.

ANT. In your bad strokes, Brutus, you give good words ;   30
Witness the hole you made in Cæsar's heart,
Crying ' Long live ! Hail, Cæsar ! '
CAS.   Antony,
The posture of your blows are yet unknown ;
But for your words, they rob the Hybla bees,
And leave them honeyless.
ANT.   Not stingless too ?   35
BRU. O yes, and soundless too ;
For you have stol'n their buzzing, Antony,
And very wisely threat before you sting.
ANT. Villains, you did not so when your vile daggers
Hack'd one another in the sides of Cæsar.   40
You show'd your teeth like apes, and fawn'd like hounds,
And bow'd like bondmen, kissing Cæsar's feet ;
Whilst damned Casca, like a cur, behind
Struck Cæsar on the neck. O you flatterers !
CAS. Flatterers ! Now, Brutus, thank yourself :   45
This tongue had not offended so to-day
If Cassius might have rul'd.
OCT. Come, come, the cause. If arguing make us sweat,
The proof of it will turn to redder drops.
Look,   50
I draw a sword against conspirators ;
When think you that the sword goes up again ?
Never till Cæsar's three and thirty wounds
Be well aveng'd, or till another Cæsar
Have added slaughter to the sword of traitors.   55
BRU. Cæsar, thou canst not die by traitors' hands,
Unless thou bring'st them with thee.
OCT.   So I hope.
I was not born to die on Brutus' sword.
BRU. O, if thou wert the noblest of thy strain,
Young man, thou couldst not die more honourable.   60
CAS. A peevish schoolboy, worthless of such honour,
Join'd with a masker and a reveller !
ANT. Old Cassius still !
OCT.   Come, Antony ; away !
Defiance, traitors, hurl we in your teeth.
If you dare fight to-day, come to the field ;   65
If not, when you have stomachs. [Exeunt OCTAVIUS, ANTONY, and
                                                    their ARMY.
CAS. Why, now, blow wind, swell billow, and swim bark !
The storm is up, and all is on the hazard.
BRU. Ho, Lucilius ! hark, a word with you.
LUCIL. My lord.   [BRUTUS and LUCILIUS converse apart.
CAS. Messala.
MES.   What says my general ?
CAS.   Messala,   70
This is my birth-day ; as this very day
Was Cassius born. Give me thy hand, Messala.
Be thou my witness that against my will,
As Pompey was, am I compell'd to set
Upon one battle all our liberties.   75

SCENE 18
*Exterior. Near Philippi.
Day.*

Lines 67–70, to 'My
Lord' and
stage direction,
omitted.

You know that I held Epicurus strong,
And his opinion ; now I change my mind,
And partly credit things that do presage.
Coming from Sardis, on our former ensign
Two mighty eagles fell ; and there they perch'd,   80
Gorging and feeding from our soldiers' hands,
Who to Philippi here consorted us.
This morning are they fled away and gone,
And in their steads do ravens, crows, and kites,
Fly o'er our heads and downward look on us   85
As we were sickly prey.   Their shadows seem
A canopy most fatal, under which
Our army lies, ready to give up the ghost.
MES. Believe not so.
CAS.   I but believe it partly ;
For I am fresh of spirit and resolv'd   90
To meet all perils very constantly.
BRU. Even so, Lucilius.
CAS.   Now, most noble Brutus,
The gods to-day stand friendly, that we may,
Lovers in peace, lead on our days to age !
But, since the affairs of men rest still incertain,   95
Let's reason with the worst that may befall.
If we do lose this battle, then is this
The very last time we shall speak together.
What are you then determined to do ?
BRU. Even by the rule of that philosophy   100
By which I did blame Cato for the death
Which he did give himself—I know not how,
But I do find it cowardly and vile,
For fear of what might fall, so to prevent
The time of life—arming myself with patience   105
To stay the providence of some high powers
That govern us below.
CAS.   Then, if we lose this battle,
You are contented to be led in triumph
Thorough the streets of Rome ?
BRU. No, Cassius, no.   Think not, thou noble Roman,   110
That ever Brutus will go bound to Rome ;
He bears too great a mind.   But this same day
Must end that work the ides of March begun,
And whether we shall meet again I know not.
Therefore our everlasting farewell take :   115
For ever and for ever farewell, Cassius !
If we do meet again, why, we shall smile ;
If not, why then this parting was well made.
CAS. For ever and for ever farewell, Brutus !
If we do meet again, we'll smile indeed ;   120
If not, 'tis true this parting was well made.
BRU. Why then, lead on.   O that a man might know
The end of this day's business ere it come !
But it sufficeth that the day will end,
| And then the end is known.   Come, ho ! away !   [*Exeunt.* | 'Come, ho! away!'
                                                                                 omitted.

SCENE II. *Near Philippi. The field of battle.*

Alarum. Enter BRUTUS *and* MESSALA.

BRU. Ride, ride, Messala, ride, and give these bills
Unto the legions on the other side.   [*Loud alarum.*
Let them set on at once ; for I perceive
But cold demeanour in Octavius' wing,
And sudden push gives them the overthrow.   5
Ride, ride, Messala ; let them all come down.   [*Exeunt.*

SCENE 19
Exterior. Near Philippi.
Day.

SCENE III. *Another part of the field.*

Alarums. Enter CASSIUS *and* TITINIUS.

CAS. O, look, Titinius, look, the villains fly !
Myself have to mine own turn'd enemy.
This ensign here of mine was turning back ;
I slew the coward, and did take it from him.
TIT. O Cassius, Brutus gave the word too early,   5
Who, having some advantage on Octavius,
Took it too eagerly   His soldiers fell to spoil,
Whilst we by Antony are all enclos'd.

SCENE 20
Exterior. Near Philippi.
Day.

Enter PINDARUS.

PIN. Fly further off, my lord, fly further off ;
Mark Antony is in your tents, my lord ;   10
Fly, therefore, noble Cassius, fly far off.
CAS. This hill is far enough.   Look, look, Titinius.
Are those my tents where I perceive the fire ?
TIT. They are, my lord.
CAS.   Titinius, if thou lovest me,
Mount thou my horse and hide thy spurs in him,   15
Till he have brought thee up to yonder troops
And here again, that I may rest assur'd
Whether yond troops are friend or enemy.
TIT. I will be here again even with a thought.   [*Exit.*
CAS. Go, Pindarus, get higher on that hill ;   20
My sight was ever thick ; regard Titinius,
And tell me what thou not'st about the field.
                                    [PINDARUS *goes up.*
This day I breathed first.   Time is come round,
And where I did begin there shall I end ;
My life is run his compass.   Sirrah, what news ?   25
PIN. [*Above.*]   O my lord !
CAS. What news ?
PIN. Titinius is enclosed round about
With horsemen that make to him on the spur ;
Yet he spurs on.   Now they are almost on him.   30
Now Titinius !   Now some light.   O, he lights too !
He's ta'en.   [*Shout.*
And hark !   They shout for joy.

CAS. Come down ; behold no more.
O, coward that I am to live so long
To see my best friend ta'en before my face ! 35

Enter PINDARUS.

Come hither, sirrah.
In Parthia did I take thee prisoner ;
And then I swore thee, saving of thy life,
That whatsoever I did bid thee do
Thou shouldst attempt it. Come now, keep thine oath ; 40
Now be a freeman, and with this good sword,
That ran through Cæsar's bowels, search this bosom.
Stand not to answer ; here, take thou the hilts ;
And when my face is cover'd, as 'tis now,
Guide thou the sword. [PINDARUS *stabs him.*
  Cæsar, thou art reveng'd, 45
Even with the sword that kill'd thee. [*Dies.*
PIN. So, I am free ; yet would not so have been,
Durst I have done my will. O Cassius !
Far from this country Pindarus shall run,
Where never Roman shall take note of him. [*Exit.*

Re-enter TITINIUS, *with* MESSALA.

MES. It is but change, Titinius ; for Octavius
Is overthrown by noble Brutus' power,
As Cassius' legions are by Antony.
TIT. These tidings will well comfort Cassius.
MES. Where did you leave him ?
TIT.   All disconsolate, 55
With Pindarus, his bondman, on this hill.
MES. Is not that he that lies upon the ground ?
TIT. He lies not like the living. O my heart !
MES. Is not that he ?
TIT.   No, this was he, Messala ;
But Cassius is no more. O setting sun, 60
As in thy red rays thou dost sink to night,
So in his red blood Cassius' day is set !
The sun of Rome is set. Our day is gone ;
Clouds, dews, and dangers come ; our deeds are done.
Mistrust of my success hath done this deed. 65
MES. Mistrust of good success hath done this deed.
O hateful error, melancholy's child,
Why dost thou show to the apt thoughts of men
The things that are not ? O error, soon conceiv'd,
Thou never com'st unto a happy birth, 70
But kill'st the mother that engend'red thee !
TIT. What, Pindarus ! Where art thou, Pindarus ?
MES. Seek him, Titinius, whilst I go to meet
The noble Brutus, thrusting this report
Into his ears. I may say ' thrusting ' it ; 75
For piercing steel and darts envenomed
Shall be as welcome to the ears of Brutus
As tidings of this sight.

TIT.   Hie you, Messala,
And I will seek for Pindarus the while.   [*Exit* MESSALA.
Why didst thou send me forth, brave Cassius ?   80
Did I not meet thy friends, and did not they
Put on my brows this wreath of victory,
And bid me give it thee ?   Didst thou not hear their shouts ?
Alas, thou hast misconstrued every thing !
But hold thee, take this garland on thy brow ;   85
Thy Brutus bid me give it thee, and I
Will do his bidding.   Brutus, come apace,
And see how I regarded Caius Cassius,
By your leave, gods.   This is a Roman's part.
Come, Cassius' sword, and find Titinius' heart.   [*Dies.*

    Alarum.   Re-enter MESSALA, *with* BRUTUS, YOUNG CATO,
             STRATO, VOLUMNIUS, *and* LUCILIUS.

BRU. Where, where, Messala, doth his body lie ?
MES. Lo yonder, and Titinius mourning it.
BRU. Titinius' face is upward.
CATO.   He is slain.
BRU. O Julius Cæsar, thou art mighty yet !
Thy spirit walks abroad and turns our swords   95
In our own proper entrails.   [*Low alarums.*
CATO.   Brave Titinius !
Look whe'r he have not crown'd dead Cassius !
BRU. Are yet two Romans living such as these ?
The last of all the Romans, fare thee well !
It is impossible that ever Rome   100
Should breed thy fellow.   Friends, I owe more tears
To this dead man than you shall see me pay.
I shall find time, Cassius, I shall find time.
Come, therefore, and to Thasos send his body.
His funerals shall not be in our camp,   105
Lest it discomfort us.   Lucilius, come ;
And come, young Cato ; let us to the field.
Labeo and Flavius set our battles on.
'Tis three o'clock ; and, Romans, yet ere night
We shall try fortune in a second fight.   [*Exeunt.*

        SCENE IV.   *Another part of the field.*
Alarum.   Enter BRUTUS, MESSALA, YOUNG CATO, LUCILIUS, *and* FLAVIUS.

BRU. Yet, countrymen, O, yet hold up your heads !
CATO. What bastard doth not ?   Who will go with me ?
I will proclaim my name about the field :
I am the son of Marcus Cato, ho !
A foe to tyrants, and my country's friend.   5
I am the son of Marcus Cato, ho !

        Enter SOLDIERS *and fight.*

BRU. And I am Brutus, Marcus Brutus, I !
Brutus, my country's friend !   Know me for Brutus !
             [*Exit.* YOUNG CATO *falls.*

SCENE 21
*Exterior. Near Philippi.
Day.*
MESSALA *does not enter.*

Lines 7–8 spoken by
LUCILIUS.
BRUTUS *does not exit.*

LUCIL. O young and noble Cato, art thou down ?
  Why, now thou diest as bravely as Titinius,   10
  And mayst be honour'd, being Cato's son.
1 SOLD. Yield, or thou diest.
LUCIL.   Only I yield to die.
| [*Offering money*]. There is so much that thou wilt kill me straight. | Stage direction
  Kill Brutus, and be honour'd in his death.   omitted.
1 SOLD. We must not.   A noble prisoner !   15

                    Enter ANTONY.

2 SOLD. Room, ho ! Tell Antony Brutus is ta'en.
1 SOLD. I'll tell the news.   Here comes the general.
  Brutus is ta'en ! Brutus is ta'en, my lord !
ANT. Where is he ?
LUCIL. Safe, Antony ; Brutus is safe enough.   20
  I dare assure thee that no enemy
  Shall ever take alive the noble Brutus.
  The gods defend him from so great a shame !
  When you do find him, or alive or dead,
  He will be found like Brutus, like himself.   25
ANT. This is not Brutus, friend ; but, I assure you,
  A prize no less in worth.   Keep this man safe;
  Give him all kindness.   I had rather have
  Such men my friends than enemies.   Go on,
  And see whe'r Brutus be alive or dead;   30
  And bring us word unto Octavius' tent
  How everything is chanc'd.   [*Exeunt.*

          SCENE V.   *Another part of the field.*   SCENE 22
                                                                 Exterior. Near Philippi.
     Enter BRUTUS, DARDANIUS, CLITUS, STRATO, *and* VOLUMNIUS. *Day.*
| BRU. Come, poor remains of friends, rest on this rock. | For 'on this rock' read
CLI. Statilius show'd the torch-light ; but, my lord,   'here'.
  He came not back.   He is or ta'en or slain.
BRU. Sit thee down, Clitus.   Slaying is the word ;
  It is a deed in fashion.   Hark thee, Clitus.   [*Whispering.*
CLI. What, I, my lord ?   No, not for all the world.
BRU. Peace, then, no words.
CLI.   I'll rather kill myself.
BRU. Hark thee, Dardanius !
DAR.   Shall I do such a deed ?
CLI. O Dardanius !
DAR. O Clitus !   10
CLI. What ill request did Brutus make to thee ?
DAR. To kill him, Clitus.   Look, he meditates.
CLI. Now is that noble vessel full of grief,
  That it runs over even at his eyes.
BRU. Come hither, good Volumnius ; list a word.   15
VOL. What says my lord ?
BRU.   Why, this, Volumnius :
  The ghost of Cæsar hath appear'd to me
  Two several times by night—at Sardis once,
  And this last night here in Philippi fields.
  I know my hour is come.

                               82

Lucilius (Andrew Hilton) and Mark Antony (Keith Michell)

The death of Cassius (David Collings), with Robert Oates as Pindarus

The death of Brutus (Richard Pasco), with Christopher Good as Clitus

VOL.   Not so, my lord.   20
BRU. Nay, I am sure it is, Volumnius.
  Thou seest the world, Volumnius, how it goes ;
  Our enemies have beat us to the pit ;   [*Low alarums.*
  It is more worthy to leap in ourselves
  Than tarry till they push us.   Good Volumnius,   25
  Thou know'st that we two went to school together ;
  Even for that our love of old, I prithee,
  Hold thou my sword-hilts whilst I run on it.
VOL. That's not an office for a friend, my lord.   [*Alarum still.*
CLI. Fly, fly, my lord ; there is no tarrying here.   30
BRU. Farewell to you ; and you ; and you, Volumnius.
  Strato, thou hast been all this while asleep ;
  Farewell to thee too, Strato.   Countrymen,
  My heart doth joy that yet in all my life
  I found no man but he was true to me.   35
  I shall have glory by this losing day,
  More than Octavius and Mark Antony
  By this vile conquest shall attain unto.
  So fare you well at once ; for Brutus' tongue
  Hath almost ended his life's history.   40
  Night hangs upon mine eyes ; my bones would rest,
  That have but labour'd to attain this hour.
                        [*Alarum.   Cry within ' Fly, fly, fly ! '*
CLI. Fly, my lord, fly.
BRU.   Hence ! I will follow.
               [*Exeunt* CLITUS, DARDANIUS, *and* VOLUMNIUS.
  I prithee, Strato, stay thou by thy lord ;
  Thou art a fellow of a good respect ;   45
  Thy life hath had some smatch of honour in it.
  Hold then my sword, and turn away thy face,
  While I do run upon it.   Wilt thou, Strato ?
STRA. Give me your hand first.   Fare you well, my lord.
BRU. Farewell, good Strato.   Cæsar, now be still.   50
  I kill'd not thee with half so good a will.
                        [*He runs on his sword, and dies.*

  Alarum.   Retreat.   Enter OCTAVIUS, ANTONY, MESSALA, LUCILIUS,
                    and the ARMY.

OCT. What man is that ?
MES. My master's man.   Strato, where is thy master ?
STRA. Free from the bondage you are in, Messala.
  The conquerors can but make a fire of him ;   55
  For Brutus only overcame himself,
  And no man else hath honour by his death.
LUCIL. So Brutus should be found.   I thank thee, Brutus,
  That thou hast prov'd Lucilius' saying true.
OCT. All that serv'd Brutus, I will entertain them.   60
  Fellow, wilt thou bestow thy time with me ?
STRA. Ay, if Messala will prefer me to you.
OCT. Do so, good Messala.
MES. How died my master, Strato ?
STRA. I held the sword, and he did run on it.   65
MES. Octavius, then take him to follow thee,

That did the latest service to my master.
ANT. This was the noblest Roman of them all.
All the conspirators save only he
Did that they did in envy of great Cæsar ;   70
He only in a general honest thought
And common good to all made one of them.
His life was gentle ; and the elements
So mix'd in him that Nature might stand up
And say to all the world ' This was a man ! '   75
OCT. According to his virtue let us use him,
With all respect and rites of burial.
Within my tent his bones to-night shall lie,
Most like a soldier, ordered honourably.
So call the field to rest, and let's away   80
To part the glories of this happy day.   [*Exeunt.*

GLOSSARY

Graham S. May

Difficult phrases are listed under the most important or most difficult word in them. If no such word stands out, they are listed under the first word.

Words appear in the form they take in the text. If they occur in several forms, they are listed under the root form (singular for nouns, infinitive for verbs).

Line references are given only when the same word is used with different meanings, and when there are puns.

Line numbers for prose passages are counted from the last numbered line before the line referred to (since the numbers given follow the lines in the First Folio and not those in this edition).

ABIDE, pay the penalty for, atone for

ABJECTS, mean-spirited, despicable things

ABOUT, go about (I i 70); 'look about you', take care

ABUSE, 'Th' abuse of greatness is . . . power', greatness is misused when the power it brings is divorced from compassion; 'the time's abuse', the corruption of the present time

ACCENTS, languages

ACCIDENTAL EVILS, chance misfortunes (see PHILOSOPHY)

ACCOUTRED, dressed, equipped

ACROSS, 'arms across', arms crossed over each other in front of the chest (i.e. in an attitude of melancholy brooding)

ACTION, gesture and bearing (of an orator, III ii 222)

ADDER, 'It is the bright day . . . adder', (proverbial)

ADDRESS'D, prepared, ready to do so

ADVANTAGE (n.), 'advantage on', advantage over; (v.), benefit us

AENEAS, OUR GREAT ANCESTOR, according to the Roman poet Virgil (*Aeneid* ii, 721), the Trojan Aeneas, who rescued his father Anchises from the burning ruins of Troy when it was being sacked by the Greeks, was the progenitor of the whole Roman nation

AFFECTION, 'forced affection', allegiance extorted under duress; 'affections sway'd', feelings ruled him

AFOOT, active, on the move

AFTER, afterwards, later (I ii 76); in accordance with (I ii 180); 'after their fashion', in their own way

AGAINST, near (I iii 20)

AGUE, acute fever (often malarial)

AIM, (capacity to) conjecture, guess (I ii 163); 'in the aim', at the very spot at which it was aimed

ALARUM, a call or signal to arms, a martial shout

ALCHEMY, the chemistry of the Middle Ages and the sixteenth century, which concentrated upon the (vain) attempt to convert base metals into gold

ALIVE, 'work alive', (i) our present concerns; (ii) matters that concern the living (and, he perhaps implies, which are more important than lamentation over the dead)

ALONG, full length, stretched out (III i 116)

AMAZE, stupefy, bewilder, confound

AMBITION'S, 'young amibition's ladder', the means by which an ambitious young man climbs towards power; 'Ambition's debt', the penalty incurred by Caesar for his ambition

AMBITIOUS, as if aspiring, towering (I iii 7)

AMISS, 'all amiss', utterly erroneously, wrongly (II ii 83)

AN, if

ANCESTORS, 'my ancestors', allusion to Lucius Junius Brutus (see BRUTUS)

ANCHISES, Aeneas' father, whom he rescued

86

from the burning ruins of Troy when it was being sacked by the Greeks

ANGEL, favourite, darling (III ii 181)

ANNOY, harm, injure

ANSWER (n.), 'My answer must be made', I shall be called to account for my words; (v.), fulfil, satisfy (V i 1); accept a challenge (V i 6); 'answer on their charge', meet them when they attack

AN'T PLEASE YOU, if it may so please you, if you wish

APACE, swiftly

APART, aside, into privacy and solitude (III i 283); to one side (V i 69 SD)

APPARENT, plain; that have been appearing

APPLY FOR, explain, interpret as

APPOINT, assign

APPREHENSIVE, possessed of reason

APT, fit, likely (II ii 97); ready, willing (III i 161); too ready, too willing (to be deceived) (V iii 68)

ARBOURS, gardens, often with herbs and flowers, or orchards

ARRIVE, reach (I ii 110)

ART, 'I have as much of this in art as you', I have as much theoretical knowledge of and acceptance of this philosophical fortitude as you

AS, 'as the Capitol', where the Capitol is (II i 111); as if (III i 99, V i 86)

ASS BEARS GOLD, allusion to the proverb, 'An ass is but an ass though laden with gold'

ASTONISH, dismay

ATÉ, according to Homer, the daughter of Zeus; according to Hesiod, the daughter of Strife. To the Greeks, Até was the personification of moral blindness or infatuation; in Shakespeare, she is the personification of strife and mischief

ATTEMPT, try to perform

AUDIENCE, a hearing

AUGHT TOWARD THE GENERAL GOOD, anything that concerns the public welfare

AUGMENTED, raised into greater power

AUGURERS, religious officials whose function it was to try and predict the future by interpreting the configuration of the entrails of sacrificial animals, the flight of birds, etc.

AWE, 'under one man's awe', in awe of a single man

AWL, small tool with a point with which holes are pierced in something (here, in pieces of leather to enable them to be sewn together)

BAIT, harass, worry (often of dogs set to worry a chained animal for sport)

BARK, small ship, boat

BARREN-SPIRITED, mean-spirited, lacking originality, ideas of his own

BARS, i.e. prison-bars

BASE (adj.), 'base matter', (i) worthless stuff used to compose and start a fire; (ii) (perhaps) a dull or plain background used as a foil or contrast to make an important detail prominent (see ILLUMINATE); 'base degrees', (i) lower rungs (of a ladder); (ii) mean, ignominious, lowly grades of office; (n.), pedestal (III ii 188)

BASIS, pedestal, base (upon which Pompey's statue stood)

BASTARD, 'What bastard doth not?', who is of so base blood that he does not?

BASTARDY, act which belies its legitimacy (i.e. shows it to be unworthy of Rome)

BATTLE, army in battle array (V i 4, V i 16, V iii 108)

BAY, howl, bark at (to 'bay the moon' was a proverbial expression to denote a futile activity)

BAY'D, (in hunting) brought to 'bay', i.e. the position of being a hunted animal finally surrounded by baying hounds, forced to turn and defend itself; 'bay'd about with many enemies', surrounded by many enemies, like so many dogs barking around their quarry (see STAKE)

BEAR, suffer (I iii 99); move (III ii 168); put up with (IV iii 85); 'bear me hard', bear ill-will towards me; 'bears Caesar hard', bears ill-will towards Caesar; 'bear no colour for the thing he is', have no plausible pretext when one considers what sort of man Caesar is now; 'bear it', behave, act (II ii 226); 'bear me a bang', receive a blow from me; 'bear his comment', be subject to criticism

BECOME, suit, befit (I ii 145, III i 203, III i 230)

BEGIN HIS FASHION, are for him the very height of fashion, are the very best that he can do

BEHAVIOURS, (good) demeanour, behaviour

BEHOLDING, obliged, indebted

BELIKE, probably, possibly, perhaps

BEND (n.), direction (of a look or glance) (I ii 123); (v.), turn, direct (II iii 5, IV iii 168); bow (obsequiously) (III i 45); 'bend his body', humbly bow (I ii 117)

BENT (n.), direction (II i 210)

BESIDES, 'know all the world besides', may everyone else know this

BEST, 'you were best', it is the best, most advisable thing for you to do

BESTOW, distribute (I iii 151); 'bestow thy time with me', i.e. agree to serve me

BETHINK, 'otherwise bethink me', change my mind

BETIMES, early, in good time (II i 116); early in the morning (IV iii 305)

BEYOND ALL USE, outside all customary experience, totally abnormal

BIG, pregnant, swelling, with grief

BILLS, decrees (IV iii 171); written orders (V ii 1)

BIRD OF NIGHT, screech-owl (believed to bring bad luck)

BLACK SENTENCE, sentence of death

BLAZE FORTH, (i) flame forth (in signification of); (ii) proclaim

BLOCKS, lumps of wood, i.e. blockheads

BLOOD, kinsmen (I i 52); 'noble bloods', (i) noble stock, families; (ii) noble dispositions, spirits; 'blood ill-temper'd, a badly balanced disposition; 'young bloods', youthful natures, constitutions

BOLD UPON, audacious in disturbing

BONDMAN, serf, a man not free but bound to serve another; a prisoner bound (i) by fetters; (ii) by a legal deed or 'bond' (see CANCEL) (I iii 101); a man bound to serve another by virtue of his being a prisoner of war (V iii 56)

BOOTLESS, without avail, in vain

BOSOMS, 'in the bosoms', aware of their secret thoughts

BOUND IN, confined to

BRANDS, pieces of burning wood, torches

BRAV'D, defied

BRAVE, noble

BRAVERY, (i) splendid display; (ii) courage (with pun on 'fearful')

BREAK WITH HIM, mention the matter to him, let him into the secret

BREED OF, ability to breed, art of breeding

BROOK'D, tolerated

BROTHER, 'Your brother too must die' (IV i 2), allusion to Lepidus' brother, Lucius Aemilius Paullus. (He was consul in 50 BC and, when Caesar was assassinated, joined the republicans. In June 43 BC he denounced Lepidus as a public enemy for having joined Antony, and the triumvirate of Antony, Caesar, and Lepidus consequently ordered his death, but he escaped to join Brutus. After Brutus' defeat he was pardoned but

refused to return to Rome, preferring to die abroad); 'brother Cassius', brother-in-law (he had married Brutus' sister Junia)

BUDGE, flinch, give way

BRUTUS, 'Brutus once', allusion to Lucius Junius Brutus, who helped to expel the Tarquins, the legendary dynasty of early Roman kings, from Rome in revenge for the rape of Lucrece by Tarquinius Sextus. Once Rome became a republic, he was one of its first consuls, in company with Tarquinius Collatinus. According to Plutarch, the Brutus of our play claimed descent from Lucius Junius Brutus. 'Old Brutus's statue', the statue of Lucius Junius Brutus

BUSINESS, labour (IV i 22)

BUSTLING RUMOUR, an agitated and confused sound, murmur

BUT, often 'only', 'merely'; except (II ii 11); 'Where Brutus may but find it', where Brutus alone will find it; 'saw his chariot but appear', caught a mere glimpse of Pompey's chariot in the distance; 'but honours', does anything other than honour; 'but for supporting', specifically on the ground that he supported

BY, 'by this', by this time (I iii 125); 'go along by him', call in at his house on your way; 'by sea and land', (i) (in token of sovereign power) over both sea and land; (ii) both when on land and when at sea (i.e. 'everywhere')

CAESAR, 'for always I am Caesar', i.e. uniquely impervious to ordinary fear

CALCULATE, prophesy (originally by mathematical or astrological methods); 'old men, fools, and children calculate', either (i) allusion to the proverbial theory that these three sorts of people are particularly capable of prophecy; or (ii) 'there are so many portents that even the very old, the very young, and idiots, are capable of interpreting them'

CALL IN QUESTION, deliberate upon

CANCEL, (in legal parlance) annul a legal agreement (see BONDMAN), i.e., 'free himself from'

CAPITOL, the temple of Jupiter Optimus Maximus, on the Saturnian or Tarpeian (later, the 'Capitoline') Hill at Rome

CAPTIVE BONDS, the fetters of captives

CARRIES, contains within him (IV iii 110)

CARRION (adj.), dead, dying, rotting

CARRIONS (n.), men who are little better than corpses

CARVE, cut up ceremoniously (perhaps an

88

allusion to the customary ceremonial carving of the deer when it had been caught and killed in a formal hunt)

CAST INTO MY TEETH, be held against me (proverbial)

CATO, Marcus Porcius Cato, uncle and father-in-law of Brutus, orator, statesman, and famous for his rigid personal moral code. In the Civil War he fought against Caesar, at first with Pompey and then, after Pompey's death, with Metellus Scipio in Africa. Eventually, rather than join the rest in Africa in their eventual surrender to Caesar, he preferred to commit suicide; 'Cato's daughter', daughter of Marcus Porcius Cato

CAUSE, the business in hand, the case being debated (term for a legal 'case') (V i 48)

CAUTELOUS, crafty, deceitful

CENSURE, judge

CEREMONY, festal adornment symbolic of Caesar's power (I i 66); prescribed rite (I ii 11); portent, omen (II i 197, II ii 13); mode of behaviour, politeness (IV ii 21)

CHAFING WITH, rubbing, raging, fretting against, dashing in anger at their restraint against

CHAIR, 'public chair', the platform (or 'pulpit') for orations

CHANC'D, happened; 'is chanc'd', has happened

CHANGE (n.), exchange of fortune (V iii 51); 'In his own change', either because of a change in his attitude towards me; (v.), change his expression (i.e. to one of fear or anger) (III i 24)

CHARACTERY OF, 'what is written upon', i.e. the significance of the furrows of sadness upon

CHARGE (n.), expenditure (IV i 9); (v.), 'things unluckily charge my fantasy', events which have occurred weigh ominously upon my imagination

CHARGES, 'their charges', those under their command, their troops

CHARM, entreat, or conjure (by means of an invocation)

CHASE, race

CHASTISEMENT, punishment

CHECK'D, rebuked, reproved

CHEW, ponder, consider

CHIDDEN TRAIN, a retinue of attendants that have been rebuked

CHOLER, 'rash choler', inflammable, explosive anger

CHOLERIC, prone to anger

CHOPT, chapped, roughened by manual labour

CINNA, (historically) Helvetius Cinna, a poet of some fame, and a friend of the poet Catullus

CLEAN FROM THE PURPOSE, in a way that is utterly different from the true meaning

CLIMATE, region, area

CLOSE (adj.), concealed, out of sight (I iii 131); (v.) make an agreement (III i 203)

CLOSET, private room, study

COBBLE YOU, mend shoes for you

COBBLER, (i) shoe-mender; (ii) bungler, bad or unskilled workman (pun)

COGNIZANCE, (i) (in heraldry) device or emblem worn by retainers; (ii) distinctive mark or badge by which to identify or remember something

COIN, make money out of, turn into money

COLOSSUS, allusion probably to the 'Colossus of Rhodes', a bronze statue of Apollo over 100 feet tall, reputed to be one of the seven wonders of the world, sculpted by Chares between 292 and 280 BC and, according to tradition, straddling the entrance to the harbour at Rhodes

COLOUR, I ii 122, (i) redness; (ii) military standard, flag (pun); 'since the quarrel Will bear no colour for the thing he is', since the quarrel has no plausible pretext when one considers what sort of man Caesar is now (see QUARREL)

COMBIN'D, joined together in one body

COME BY, get possession of (II i 169); obtain (II i 259)

COMMEND ME, deliver my greeting, my compliments

COMMENT, 'bear his comment', be subject to criticism

COMMIT, entrust

COMMONS, common people (III ii 130); 'in commons', on public pasturelands

COMPACT, agreement

COMPANION, fellow (term of contempt)

COMPASS, full circuit, revolution

COMPLEXION OF THE ELEMENT, visible appearance, condition, of the sky

CONCAVE SHORE, overhanging, hollowed-out, banks

CONCEIT, I iii 162, (i) judge, understand; (ii) express by means of a metaphor (pun); judge, conceive (III i 193)

CONCEPTIONS ONLY PROPER TO,

thoughts which should strictly concern only, belong exclusively to

CONDEMN'D TO HAVE, accused and criticised adversely for having

CONDITION, physical constitution (II i 236); mental disposition (II i 254); 'make conditions', manage affairs, or perhaps, prescribe duties to subordinates, instruct others how they should behave

CONFERENCE, debate, argument (I ii 188); conversation (IV ii 17)

CONFINES, regions

CONFOUNDED WITH, stunned, amazed, by

CONJOINTLY MEET, occur together, coincide

CONJURE, use them in spells to raise up spirits (I ii 146); 'conjur'd up', raised (of a spirit)

CONN'D, studied, committed to memory

CONQUEST, victory (I i 33)

CONSORTED, accompanied

CONSTANT, resolute (III i 60, III i 72); calm, resolute (III i 22)

CONSTANTLY, resolutely

CONSTRUE, interpret (I iii 34); elucidate (II i 307); 'construe any further', interpret as having any further significance

CONSUM'D IN CONFIDENCE, destroyed by over-confidence

CANTAGION, poisonous influence

CONTENT, 'be you content', set your mind at rest; 'be content', keep calm (IV ii 41)

CONTRIVE, conspire, plot

CONTRIVER, plotter, intriguer (and see SHREWD)

CONTROVERSY, 'hearts of controversy', hearts eager to compete against both each other and the waves

CORPORAL MOTION, physical movements

CORSE, corpse

COUCHINGS, bowings

COUNCIL, 'in council', are debating, deliberating, together (see GENIUS)

COUNSEL, private, secret thought; 'keep counsel', keep a secret

COUNTENANCE, favour, approval (perhaps, 'his face used as a figure-head') (I iii 159)

COUNTERS, derogatory term for coins (often = imitation coins, worthless tokens, used for making calculations)

COURSE, running-race (part of the Lupercalian celebrations) (I ii 4, I ii 25); 'for the course', prepared for the running-race

COVERT MATTERS, hidden things (i.e. secret plans of the enemy)

COWARD LIPS . . . COLOUR FLY, his lips went pale (lost their rightful and honourable redness through fear) as if they were a cowardly soldier deserting his standard or flag ('colour') and fleeing

CRAVES, demands, necessitates

CREDIT (n.), reputation, capacity to be believed and trusted; (v.), believe

CRESTS, the ridge of a horse's neck (when held high, considered to be the sign of a spirited horse)

CROSS (adj.), forked, zig-zag; (v.), contradict, oppose, argue with; 'I do not cross you', I am not being merely perverse in contradicting you

CROUCH, bow

CULL OUT A HOLIDAY, pick, select this as a holiday (from the mass of working-days)

CUMBER, burden, afflict

CUR, dog

CURSE, 'sterile curse', cursed affliction of sterility

CURTSIES, bows

CUSTOM, (insensibility stemming from) familiarity with

CUT OFF SOME CHARGE, reduce some of the expenditure

CYNIC, rude fellow (particularly one who is disposed to rail and find fault)

DAMN, condemn (here, 'to death')

DANGER, 'do danger', create mischief, harm

DARE, challenge, defy (II i 265)

DEAR, keenly, dearly (III ii 114)

DEARER (adj.), more precious (IV iii 101); (adv.), more keenly (III i 197)

DEATH, 'wrath in death', see WRATH

DEBT, see AMBITION'S DEBT

DEFENCE, the ability to defend ourselves

DEGREES, (i) steps, rungs (of a ladder); (ii) stages (in the ascent to power), grades of office

DELIVER, declare, communicate, to (III i 182)

DEMAND OF, issue a challenge to

DEMEANOUR, 'cold demeanour', lack of spirit in fighting

DEW, i.e. refreshment (II i 230)

DIE, i.e. suffer death-like agonies of fear and apprehension (II ii 32)

DIFFERENCE, 'passions of some difference', emotions which conflict with each other to no small extent

DIGEST, listen to, accept, and ponder (I ii 300); swallow (IV iii 47)

DIGNITIES, honours, high offices

DINT, stroke, blow; impression

DIRECTLY, to the point, straightforwardly (I i 12, III iii 9); III iii 19–20, pun on (i) straightforwardly; (ii) in a straight line

DISCLOS'D, found out, brought to light

DISCOMFORT US, dishearten our troops

DISCOVER, reveal (I ii 69); recognise, find the identity of (II i 75)

DISHONOUR SHALL BE HUMOUR, your dishonourable action, your insults to me, shall be taken by me as a mere harmless caprice

DISHONOURABLE GRAVES, i.e. the only option open to us now is death, and even that (and hence, our graves) would be dishonourable, because we are no longer free men

DISPOS'D, 'from that it is dispos'd', away from its natural inclination

DISROBE, remove the ornaments which cover

DISTRACT, 'fell distract', became suddenly greatly troubled in mind

DO, 'to do', to be done (II i 326); 'What should the wars have to do with these jigging fools?', what possible function can such rhyming idiots fulfil in war?; 'do kiss', i.e. does rise to

DOGS OF WAR, i.e. the full bestial violence of war

DOUBT, suspect, are suspicious of (II i 132)

DRACHMAS, Greek silver coins

DRAWING DAYS OUT, prolonging life

DRAWN UPON A HEAP, huddled together

DROPPING, raining

DULL, obtuse, stupid, lacking spirit

EASE OURSELVES . . . SLAND'ROUS LOADS, remove some of the burden of reproach which may be directed towards us (i.e. by laying the blame for unpopular acts on Lepidus)

ELEMENT, sky (I iii 128)

ELEMENTS, originally, 'the four elements (earth, air, fire and water) out of which, it was believed, all matter was composed'; here, however, the term is used loosely to denote the four 'humours' (phlegm, blood, melancholy and choler), the four chief fluids of the body, the relative proportions of which, it was thought, determined a person's mental and physical disposition

EMPTY, unburdened

EMULATION, envious rivalry

ENEMY, 'Caesar was ne'er so much your enemy', allusion to Ligarius' taking sides against Caesar in the Civil War (see LIGARIUS)

ENFORC'D, overstressed, exaggerated (III ii 39); strained (IV ii 21); IV iii 111, (i) subjected to pressure; (ii) struck violently (proverbial)

ENFRANCHISEMENT, recall from exile (III i 57); release from bondage (III i 81)

ENGAG'D, pledged

ENGAGEMENTS, commitments

ENGRAFTED, firmly attached

ENLARGE, expatiate upon, recount in full

ENROLL'D, recorded in the archives

ENSIGN, military standard, banner (V i 79); standard-bearer (V iii 3) (see IT)

ENTERTAIN THEM, take them into my service

ENTIRE, 'man entire', whole man (all four 'parts', i.e. 'quarters')

ENVIOUS, spiteful, malicious

ENVY, (personal) malice, hatred

EPICURUS, Greek philosopher (c. 340–c. 270 BC) who posited a materialistic physics. His followers believed that the gods were indifferent to human affairs, and hence believed that there was no validity in omens or portents

EREBUS, Hell (strictly, the dark area beneath the earth through which the souls of the dead were believed to pass on their way to Hades)

ERUPTIONS, unnatural events, outbreaks of occurrences outside the normal bounds of nature

ET TU, BRUTE?, And you too, Brutus? (Latin)

ETERNAL, term of extreme abhorrence, perhaps 'infernal' or 'everlastingly damned'

EVEN (adj.), straightforward, steadfast, balanced (II i 133); level (V i 17); (n), evening

EVER NOTE, always observe

EXALTED, 'most exalted', highest; 'exalted with', raised up to

EXCEPTED, omitted (legal phrase, associated with the legal processes concerned with land-tenure)

EXHALATIONS, meteors (which were thought to be vapours emitted by the earth when under the influence of the sun, and then ignited by the sun's heat)

EXIGENT, emergency, crisis

EXORCIST, one who conjures up (and exorcises) spirits

EXPEDITION, swift march

EXTENUATED, understated, depreciated

EYE, 'have an eye to', keep watch on; 'had his eyes', i.e. (i) were not blind, (ii) 'possessed the eyes of the man who spoke of Brutus', and hence, 'regarded Caesar in the same way (as the one who spoke of Brutus)'

FACE, outward show (V i 10); 'face of men', i.e. the sorrowful, anxious expression on men's faces (in response to Caesar's tyranny)

FACTION, group of conspirators

FACTIOUS, 'be factious for', form a party, faction, to effect the

FACULTIES, 'preformed faculties', characteristics with which they were originally endowed

FAIN, willingly

FALL, happen (III i 244); lower, let fall (IV ii 26); 'Falls shrewdly to the purpose', turns out to correspond dangerously and accurately with what really happens; 'fell a-shouting', began to shout

FALLING SICKNESS, epilepsy (with some such implicit meaning as 'dishonourable subservience', or 'we are diseased and likely to fall from prosperity beneath Caesar's arrogance', I ii 255)

FALSE, out of tune (IV iii 289)

FAM'D WITH, celebrated for

FAMILIAR INSTANCES, signs, proofs, of friendship

FANTASY, figments of the imagination; imagination (III iii 2)

FAR, probably 'further' (III ii 167)

FASHION (n.), habitual manner, mode of behaviour (IV iii 133); 'after their fashion', in their own way; (v.), 'Fashion it thus', let us put it this way, use this line of argument; 'fashion him', mould him, persuade him to join us

FATAL, presaging death

FAVOUR, appearance (I iii 129); appearance, countenance (II i 76); 'outward favour', external appearance, face

FAWN, affect a servile fondness

FEAR, 'no fear in', nothing to fear from

FEARFUL, inspiring fear, terrible; 'fearful bravery', either (i) a splendid show which would inspire fear; or (ii) a splendid show which masks their underlying fear

FELL (adj.), cruel, terrible

FELLOW, equal; term of address to inferiors or servants (III ii 262)

FERRET, red (like those of a ferret), bloodshot (with anger or resentment)

FIELD, troops (V v 80)

FIGURES, figments of the imagination, imaginings

FIND OUT, look for (I iii 134)

FIRE (n.), 'swallow'd fire', according to Plutarch, Portia choked herself to death by swallowing burning coals; 'As fire drives out fire, so pity pity', (proverbial), as one fire extinguishes another (by burning away all the available combustible fuel), so pity for the general wrong of Rome must extinguish pity for the private wrong suffered by Caesar; 'but make a fire of him', can only burn him on a funeral pyre (not capture him alive); (v.), work a powerful effect upon

FIT, i.e. of shivering when suffering from a fever (such as malaria) (I ii 120)

FLEERING, sneering, gibing

FLINT, i.e. with which to strike a piece of steel to generate a spark, light tinder, and, in turn, light the candle

FLOOD, 'great flood', allusion to the classical legend that Zeus, enraged with the degeneracy of mankind, flooded the earth, destroying all human beings except the pious couple Deucalion, king of Phthia, and his wife Pyrrha

FLOURISH (n.), fanfare of trumpets

FLOURISH'D, (i) brandished a sword; (ii) swaggered, triumphed

FOND, so foolish as

FOOLS, congenital idiots (I iii 65)

FOR, as for (II i 181); beneficial, good for (II i 235); to indulge, comply with (II ii 56)

FORCE, 'of force', of necessity

FORM, pose, pretended demeanour (I ii 298); external appearance (IV ii 40); 'right form of war', proper military fashion, battle order; 'forms', benches (III ii 260)

FORMAL CONSTANCY, dignified composure

FORMER ENSIGN, foremost banner, forward military standard

FORTH, go forth (II ii 10, III i 120); 'forth of doors', out of doors (III iii 3)

FREE, at liberty to range freely (II i 79)

FREEDOM OF REPEAL, permission to be recalled from banishment

FREEMAN, a man released from bondage, in this case from bondage to Cassius and, by fulfilling it, from bondage to his oath

FRET, (i) interlace, adorn with an interlacing pattern; (ii) gnaw, wear away

FROM, away from (I ii 309, III ii 165); different, diverging from (I iii 35, II i 196); 'from quality and kind', act in a way which is contrary to their proper natures

FURY, mad tumult, strife

GALLANT, splendid

GAMESOME, (i) sport-loving; (ii) frivolous

GAZE, gape, look dazed

GENERAL, II i 12, i.e. a reason of a more general, public, nature (as distinct from the 'personal cause' of line 11), consideration of the common public good; public (III ii 89); 'in a general honest thought And common good to all', with an honourable intention motivated by a care for the community, and concern for the good of all Romans

GENIUS . . . COUNCIL, the Genius (either (i) 'attendant or guardian spirit allotted to each man at birth', or (ii) 'the reasonable soul' (the only immortal part of man's mind, according to the old, ultimately Aristotelian, psychology)) and the mortal instruments (either (i) 'the bodily powers' ('mortal' as subject to extinction upon death, unlike the Genius), or (ii) 'the passions') are debating and deliberating together

GENTLE, good, kind; noble, magnanimous (V v 73)

GENTLENESS, courtesy, affability

GHASTLY, spectre-like, pale with fear

GIVEN, 'well given', well-disposed

GLANCED AT, hinted at, alluded to

GLASS, mirror; 'bears with glasses', i.e. bears could be confused by the reflection of their own image in a 'glass' (mirror)

GO TO, dismissive exclamation, e.g. 'Come now'

GOES, 'how it goes', how events are taking shape now

GONE, walked (I i 27)

GOWN, dressing-gown

GRACE (n.), 'do grace to', pay respect to, honour; (v.), do honour to; do honour to, adorn (III i 121); respect (III ii 57)

GRACIOUS, virtuous, holy

GREETS, 'He greets me well', he sends his greetings by a good man

GRIEFS, grievances, grudges (I iii 118, III ii 213, IV ii 46)

GROWING UPON, encroaching upon

GRUDGE, ill-will

HA', have (I iii 19)

HALF, i.e. wife (II i 274)

HAND, 'bear too stubborn and too strange a hand Over', (metaphor from horsemanship, describing the manner of holding the reins) you exercise too severe, repressive, and hostile a control over your behaviour towards; 'several hands', many different styles of handwriting; 'my hand', here is my hand upon it (I iii 117); 'in hand', in preparation (I iii 129, II i 316); 'at the hand of', from (II i 58); 'have any hand at all About', have anything to do with, role to play in (III i 249–50); 'at hand', (i) near (IV ii 4, V i 4); (ii) at the start (IV ii 23)

HAPPY TIME, 'in very happy time', at a very opportune, favourable, moment

HART, stag (with pun on 'heart')

'HAVOC!', (in battle) the signal to allow unrestrained slaughter and pillage. This order could only be given by a monarch – hence Até has 'a monarch's voice'

HAZARD, 'on the hazard', at stake (originally an image from gambling)

HEAD, 'make head', raise a force

HEALTH, i.e. safety, welfare (IV iii 36)

HEAVY, sad, melancholy (II i 275); sleepy (IV iii 254)

HEDGE ME IN, prescribe limits to my freedom of action

HEED, 'take heed', pay careful attention to, watch carefully

HENCE, go from this place (IV iii 228)

HIDE, 'Chastisement . . . head', punishment is therefore omitted (for Cassius as well as for other men) (IV iii 16)

HIE, hasten, hurry

HIGH, important (I ii 170)

HIGH-SIGHTED, (i) supercilious, arrogant; (ii) looking downward, able to see from a great height (like a falcon – see RANGE); (iii) ambitious

HILTS, hilt

HINDS, (i) (mere) female deer; (ii) peasants, low-born men; (iii) servants

HIS, (often) its

HISTORY, narrative record

HOLD, consider (I ii 78); remains the same (perhaps 'remains sane') (I ii 290); 'Here take!', or 'wait!' (I iii 117); delay, detain (IV iii 263); 'holds on', retains, keeps; 'held Epicurus strong', was a firm believer in and follower of Epicurus (allusion to the fact that the followers of Epicurus, the Greek philosopher, felt there to be no validity in omens or portents, for they believed that the gods were indifferent to human affairs); 'hold thee', wait (V iii 85)

HOLES, i.e. concealed pits (into which they would fall and become trapped)

HOLLOW, insincere

HONEST, honourable

HONESTY, integrity, honour

HONEY-HEAVY DEW, overpoweringly sweet refreshment

HONOURS (n.), 'our large honours', honourable offices which it is in our power to bestow (IV iii 25); (v.), gives an air of respectability to (IV iii 15)

HOOTED, shouted in disapprobation (I ii 242)

HORSE IN GENERAL, all the mounted soldiers

HOT AT HAND, spirited and lively at the start

HOUR, i.e. of death (V v 20, V v 42)

HOW?, i.e., perhaps, 'what are you doing here?' (II i 312)

HOWEVER, no matter how, in spite of the fact that (I ii 298)

HUMOUR (n.), disposition; momentary mood, whim (II i 250); moisture, dampness (II i 262); 'give his humour the true bent', influence his disposition and turn it in the right direction; 'for thy humour', to indulge, comply with, your whim; 'dishonour shall be humour', your dishonourable acts, your insults to me, shall be taken by me as mere harmless caprice; 'rash humour', irascible temperament; 'know his humour', recognise his eccentric disposition; (v.), influence, subtly manipulate by persuasion (I ii 314)

HURTLED, clattered, clashed

HYBLA BEES, 'rob the Hybla bees', outdo in sweetness the honey of the bees of the town of Hybla in Sicily, proverbially famous for its honey (Cassius is alluding to Antony's profession of allegiance to the conspirators just after the death of Caesar)

IDES OF MARCH, the fifteenth of March

IDLE BED, (i) bed in which he lies idle; (ii) (perhaps) unused bed

ILL-TEMPER'D, 'blood ill-temper'd, a badly-balanced disposition; 'I was ill-temper'd too', I was also badly balanced in temperament (and perhaps 'peevish', 'cross', 'bad-tempered')

ILLUMINATE, (i) throw light upon (by burning); (ii) serve as a dull background (as in the 'illumination' or preparation with elaborate pictorial embellishment, of written manuscripts) to serve as a foil, contrast, to make Caesar appear prominent

IMAGES, representations, statues, of Caesar, or of various deities

IMITATIONS, second-hand ideas

IMPOSSIBLE, i.e. which seem impossible to overcome (II i 325)

IMPROVE, make good use of

INCORPORATE (v.), make one body of us

INCORPORATE TO, bound up, united, in league, with

INDIFFERENT, a matter of indifference

INDIFFERENTLY, (i) impassively, with indifference; (ii) (perhaps) impartially

INDIRECTION, irregular, unjust, means

INFIRMITY, illness (i.e. epilepsy)

INSTANCES, marks, signs, proofs

INSTIGATIONS, incitements, goadings

INSUPPRESSIVE, indomitable, insuppressible

INTERMIT, delay, withhold

IS, often, with verbs describing physical motion, 'has'

ISSUE, offspring (III ii 137); 'cruel issue', the result of the cruelty

IT, i.e. the standard, banner (V iii 4)

ITCHING PALM, a covetous hand, a mercenary streak

JADES, poor, vicious, horses

JEALOUS, doubtful (I ii 162); 'jealous on', suspicious of

JIGGING, rhyming, versifying

JUST, right, exactly so (I ii 54)

KEEP, (i) associate (I ii 310); keep to (V i 3); 'keep counsel', keep a secret

KERCHIEF, cloth used to cover the head, often in Elizabethan England taken to be a sign of sickness, i.e. 'wear a kerchief' = be ill

KILL, (let us, therefore,) kill (II i 34)

KILLING, being killed (IV iii 148)

KIND, nature (I iii 64); 'as his kind', as is its nature

KISS, i.e. rise to (I i 61)

KNAVE, servant, menial, perhaps 'rascal' (I i 15); boy (IV iii 239, IV iii 267)

KNOT, party of men bound together in a conspiracy

KNOW, recognise, indulge (IV iii 134); 'know all the world besides', may everyone else know that; 'know you Brutus', recognise you as Brutus

LAST, i.e. conclusion (of my speech) (III ii 12)

LATE, 'of late', recently; 'I do observe you now of late', I have recently been watching you closely; 'Vexed I am Of late', I have recently been troubled

LAUGHTER, object of laughter, laughing-stock (i.e. one not to be taken seriously), source of laughter, object of ridicule

LAW OF CHILDREN, mere childish fickleness, capriciousness

LEADEN, i.e. blunt (III i 174)

LEAGUES, a 'league' was a measure of distance, varying from country to country, but approximately three miles in length

LEARN OF, take instruction from

LEAVE (n.), 'By your leave, gods', Titinius asks of the gods permission to commit suicide because, in so doing, he is knowingly cutting short the span of life allotted to him by them; (v.), 'leave you so', leave it at that

LEISURE, 'at your best leisure', whenever best suits you

LET, 'be let blood', i.e. be killed (allusion to the contemporary practice of curing or alleviating illness by making the patient bleed); 'let slip', unleash

LETHE, a river in Hades, the water of which induced forgetfulness. Hence 'Lethe' was often used to mean 'oblivion', and here means 'life-blood'

LIABLE, 'liable to', susceptible, subject to (I ii 199); 'to my love is liable', is subject to, subordinate to, controlled by, my affection for you

LIEF, 'had as lief not be', would wish just as much to be dead (perhaps with a pun on the sounds of 'as live' and 'as lief')

LIES, lodges (for the night) (III i 287)

LIGARIUS, 'Caius Ligarius', historically Quintus Ligarius. According to Plutarch, he had been charged before Caesar with taking sides with Pompey against Caesar in the Civil War. Caesar discharged him, but Ligarius was bitterly resentful for having been thus endangered by what he saw to be Caesar's tyrannical power (*see* II ii 111–13)

LIGHT, alight, fall; dismount (V iii 31)

LIKE, likely (I ii 175, I ii 253); 'like is not the same', apparent similarity may conceal a radical difference; 'like himself', true to his own noble nature; 'their likes', those which are similar to them; 'like to', much like

LIMB OF, i.e. a mere subsidiary, dependant upon

LIMITATION, 'in a limited way' or 'for a limited period' (legal term for the period specified for the continuance of an estate)

LION IN THE CAPITOL, (i) allusion to the lion mentioned by Casca (I iii 20); (ii) perhaps an allusion to the lions kept at this time in the Tower of London, and considered to be one of the sights of London

LIST, hear

LISTEN, hear (IV i 41)

LIVELONG, intensive form of 'long', i.e. 'livelong day' = even for the whole length of the day

LOADS, 'sland'rous loads', burdens of reproach or disgrace

LODGE (v.), encamp

LOOK (v.), 'look you', be sure you; 'look about you', take care; 'he looks quite through the deeds of men', his insight pierces through to the motives which underlie men's actions

LOTTERY, chance (i.e. according to the tyrant's whim)

LOVE TO, interest in, concern for

LOVER, dear friend

LOW-CROOKED, bending low

LOWLINESS, (affectation, pretence, of) humility

LOWLY COURTESIES, humble obeisances

LUPERCAL, 'feast of Lupercal', a feast of expiation and purification in honour of Lupercus, the god of shepherds

LUSTY, vigorous

MACE, a staff carried by the sheriff's officer, a symbol of his office, with which he touched the shoulders of those whom he wished to arrest

MAIN OPINION, strongly-held opinion

MAKE, 'make our purpose necessary', make it clear that our action was motivated by necessity; 'make sick', i.e. kill; 'makes to', advances towards, approaches; 'make forth', go forward; 'made', made certain (IV i 44)

MALICE, 'Our arms in strength of malice', our arms, although they must seem to you to be strong in enmity

MARK, listen attentively to (I ii 126, III ii 112); consider it to be worthy of serious attention (I ii 235); closely observe (II iii 2, III i 18)

MARRY, indeed, to be sure

MART, deal, traffic, in

MASKER, one who takes part in a masked ball, or in a theatrical show performed by actors wearing masks

95

MATTERS, 'tradesman's matters, nor women's matters', (perhaps a topical allusion to Dekker's play *The Shoemaker's Holiday*, performed in 1599, in which there is a master-shoemaker Simon Eyre, who meddles with 'tradesman's matters' and 'women's matters')

MEAN OF DEATH, means, way, of dying

MEANS, capacities, resources (II i 158); supplies, resources (IV iii 198); 'By means whereof', as a result of which (i.e. my mistake)

MECHANICAL, artisans, craftsmen

MEDDLE, (i) interfere; (ii) have sexual relations with; (pun)

MEET (adj.), suitable, fitting

MELANCHOLY'S CHILD, the product of melancholy (which tends to make the sufferers from it imagine non-existent evils)

MELTING, yielding to emotion, tender

MEMORY, as a memorial, to remind them of him

MEND, (i) repair; (ii) reform; (pun)

MENDER, (i) repairer; (ii) reformer; (pun)

MERELY, entirely

MERRY, in good spirits

METAL, (i) disposition; (ii) metal (the substance); 'basest metal', their most mean disposition (with a pun on 'least precious metal' which is picked up in 'guiltiness', a pun on 'gilt')

METELLUS CIMBER, (historically) Lucius Tillius Cimber, once a friend of Caesar, who eventually joined the conspiracy against him

METTLE, disposition; courage (IV ii 24); 'quick mettle', lively of disposition (Cassius takes this to mean 'of ready courage', I ii 296)

MIND, opinion, intention, mental faculties; opinion (II iii 4); 'have mind upon', take heed for

MIRTH, source, object, of mirth

MISCHIEFS, injuries (which they would wish to do us)

MISCHIEVOUS, harmful

MISCONSTRUED, misinterpreted

MISTOOK, misunderstood

MISTRUST OF MY SUCCESS, fear of the outcome of my mission (*see* SUCCESS)

MOCK, scornful, sarcastic, remark

MODESTLY, without exaggeration

MODESTY, moderation

MONARCH'S, i.e. powerful, all-commanding (*see* 'HAVOC!')

MONSTROUS, unnatural, abnormal

MORTAL INSTRUMENTS, see GENIUS

MORTIFIED, deadened

MOTHER, i.e. 'melancholy' and 'Cassius who felt the melancholy fit' (V iii 71)

MOTION, promptings, impulse (II i 64)

MOVE, persuade; urge (I ii 167); 'well mov'd', easily susceptible to persuasion

MUCH, 'that were much he should', that would be too much to expect from him

MUSIC, 'he hears no music', allusion to the Platonic belief that the man whose mind is harmoniously balanced takes a natural delight in the harmonies of music, and hence that he who dislikes music should not be trusted, being only 'fit for treasons, stratagems, and spoils' (*The Merchant of Venice*, V i 85)

MUTINY, uproar, tumult, riot

NAME, 'my name', a conceited periphrasis for 'I'

NAPKINS, handkerchiefs

NATIVE SEMBLANCE, natural (i.e. true) appearance

NATURE, 'the nature of', something like, a kind of

NAUGHTY, worthless, good-for-nothing

NEAT'S LEATHER, ox or cow hide

NECESSARY, seem to have been clearly motivated by necessity (II i 178)

NECESSITIES, 'our necessities', those things which are of urgent and supreme importance to us

NEEDS MUST, must of necessity

NERVII, allusion to Caesar's hard-won and important victory over the Nervii (according to Plutarch, 'the stoutest warriors' of all Belgae) at Sambre, in the winter of 57 B C, during the Gallic Wars. So important was the victory, in which Caesar himself showed conspicuous and exemplary bravery, that the Senate ordered the Roman people to hold feasts and processions on a hitherto unparalleled scale. (Historically, Antony was not present at the battle)

NEW-ADDED, reinforced

NEW-FIR'D, new-kindled with enthusiasm, hope, courage

NICE, trivial

NIGGARD (v.), stint, put off with a short allowance

NIGHT, i.e. sleep (II i 99)

NIGHT-GOWN, dressing-gown

NO, 'no fear in', nothing to fear from; 'or no', or not

NOD ON, nod at

NORTHERN STAR, the pole star (which alone of the stars remains unmoving in the heavens)

NOTED, stigmatised, publicly branded with disgrace

NOTHING JEALOUS, not at all doubtful

NOTICE OF, information, news, about

OBSERVE, be obsequious to (IV iii 45); 'I do observe you now of late', I have recently been watching you closely

OCCUPATION, 'a man of any occupation', (i) a man engaged in a handicraft, a tradesman; (ii) a man of action

O'ERSHOT MYSELF, gone further than I intended

O'ERSWAY, persuade him to the contrary

O'ERWATCHED, exhausted by staying awake too long

OF, about (I ii 70); by (II i 156); from (IV iii 3, IV iii 54); 'of force', of necessity

OFFAL, wood chips (thrown off when working wood)

OFFENCE, hurt, harm, injury (IV iii 199); 'sick offence', harmful injury

OFFERING, sacrificial animal (whose entrails would be examined for any abnormality which could be interpreted as an omen)

OFFICES, positions, posts, of authority (IV iii 11)

OLYMPUS, the mountain in Thessaly which was thought to be the home of the Greek gods; 'lift up Olympus', try to move Mount Olympus, i.e. try to achieve the impossible

OMITTED, if neglected

ON, at (I ii 118); over (V iii 6)

ONCE, at some time (IV iii 189)

O'NIGHTS, 'such as sleep o'nights', the sort of people who can sleep at night (i.e., who are undisturbed by anxieties)

ON'T, of it (i.e. the news that Casca has joined the conspiracy)

OPE, open

OPINION, reputation (II i 145)

ORCHARD, (probably) garden

ORDER, progress, manner of taking place (I ii 25); ceremony (III i 231)

ORDER'D HONOURABLY, treated with honour

ORDINANCE, usual natural behaviour (as ordained by divine providence)

ORDINARY, (i) commonplace; (ii) (perhaps) customary, ritual; (iii) (perhaps) fit for a common tavern (known as an 'ordinary')

ORTS, scraps of left-over food

OTHER, 'gentler than other', more gently (i.e. less willingly) than on the previous occasion

OUT, I i 16, (i) angry; (ii) out at heel, with worn-out shoes; (pun)

OUTWARD, external; 'outward favour', outside appearance, countenance

OVER, in turn (II i 112)

OVER-EARNEST, excessively serious

PALM, branch or leaf of the palm tree, used as a symbol of victory, hence 'bear the palm', carry off the victor's prize

PALTER, deceive, equivocate

PART (n.), proper function, business (I iii 54); (v.), divide, share (III ii 4, V v 81)

PASS, pass through (I i 43); pass onwards (I ii 24)

PASSION, feeling (I ii 40, I ii 48); sorrow (III i 284)

PEEVISH, silly, childish

PERILS, 'open perils surest answered', clearly manifest dangers dealt with with the greatest safety

PHANTASMA, nightmare

PHILOSOPHY, 'your philosophy', allusion to Brutus' profession of the austere Stoic philosophy, with its emphasis on patient endurance won through the practice of indifference to pleasure and pain, chance misfortunes ('accidental evils'), and the repression of emotion; 'that philosophy', allusion to the Stoical philosophy, to which Brutus conceived himself as adhering, one of whose tenets was that suicide was 'cowardly' and 'vile'

PHYSICAL, healthy

PIECE IT OUT, complete, fill out, augment, it (i.e. the abbreviated message)

PIT, (i) pit into which animals are driven in order to trap them; (ii) grave

PITCH, height to which a falcon soars before swooping upon its prey; 'fly an ordinary pitch', soar to the same height as, behave in the same way as, other men

PITIFUL, full of pity

PLACE, status as your wife (II i 269); office, position (III ii 42); 'give place', (i) make room, get out of the way (III i 10); (ii) give way, surrender (IV iii 144); 'holy place', i.e. in the temple-area

PLEBEIANS, common people of Rome

PLUCK, pull; 'pluck'd about', pulled down

97

around; 'pluck down', tear loose; 'pluckt me ope', wrenched open

PLUTUS' MINE, the mine of Plutus, the god (and personification) of wealth, (often confused with Pluto, god of the underworld)

POINT UPON, (in astrology), direct a malignant influence towards

POMPEY, Gnaeus Pompeius Magnus, Pompey the Great, Caesar's former rival in the Civil War, over whom Caesar was victorious at the battle of Pharsalia in 48 BC, and who was later assassinated; 'as Pompey was', allusion to the fact that, at the battle of Pharsalia at which he was defeated by Caesar, he had been forced to fight against his better judgement; 'Pompey's porch', the portico of the theatre built by Pompey in 55 BC

POOR, 'none so poor', even the meanest person is not mean enough

PORCH, see POMPEY'S PORCH

PORTENTOUS UNTO, ominous, bearing ill omens, for

POST, ride with speed

POSTURE, nature (actually the technical term for the position of a weapon in arms drill or war)

POWER, body of armed men, armed force (IV i 42, V iii 52)

PRACTICE (n.), experience (IV iii 31)

PRAETOR, Roman judge of high rank; 'praetor's chair', the seat in which the chief Roman magistrate would sit to settle disputes brought before him

PREFER, offer, present (III i 28); recommend (V v 62)

PRE-FORMED, originally ordained

PREPARE WITHIN, i.e. prepare the wine indoors

PRE-ORDINANCE AND FIRST DECREE, what has been preordained and decreed from the very first

PRESENT (adj.), immediate (II ii 5); (n.), present time, moment (I ii 165)

PRESENTLY, immediately

PRESS (n.), throng, crowd; (v), throng, crowd around

PREVAIL, succeed, successfully persuade you

PREVENT, forestall by taking preventive action; we must take preventive action (II i 28)

PREVENTION, being forestalled, thwarted, by anticipatory action (II i 85); that we may be forestalled by anticipatory action (III i 19)

PRICK, incite, spur (II i 124); mark upon a list (with a tick or small pin-prick), i.e. include (III i 217, IV i 1, IV i 3, IV i 16)

PRITHEE, beg you

PROCEEDING, advancement

PRODIGIES, awesome, portentous, phenomena

PRODIGIOUS GROWN, who has become ominous, supernaturally threatening

PROFESS MYSELF, make profession of friendship

PROGRESS OF THE STARS, the regular movement of the stars across the sky (as the earth rotates)

PROMIS'D FORTH, 'am promis'd forth', have promised to dine elsewhere

PROOF, practical test (V i 49); 'a common proof', a matter of common knowledge generally experienced; 'strong proof', a severe test

PROPER, 'As proper men . . . neat's leather', (proverbial), as fine, handsome, men as ever walked; 'own proper', very own (emphatic, as 'proper' = 'own'); 'proper to', peculiar to, concerning only; belonging exclusively to

PROPERTY, (mere) tool, possession

PROSCRIPTION, decree of condemnation to banishment or (as here) death

PROTEST, proclaim

PROTESTER, one who merely professes affection

PROVIDENCE, 'stay the providence of', await and endure the fate ordained us by

PUBLIC, III ii 7, (i) concerning the public good; (ii) given in public; 'public chair', the platform (or 'pulpit') for orators; 'public leave to speak', permission to speak publicly

PUBLIUS, (historically) Antony had no such nephew, although his uncle Lucius Caesar was proscribed (i.e. placed on the public list of those who were to be condemned, if caught, to death) by the Triumvirate of Antony, Caesar and Lepidus

PUISSANT, powerful

PULPIT, raised platform (perhaps an allusion to the contemporary open-air pulpits)

PURGERS, healers (originally, those who professed to cure a patient by bleeding and purging him)

PURPLED, stained with blood

PURPOSE, meaning, import (I iii 35); design, intention (II i 225); 'falls shrewdly to the purpose', turns out to accord with unpleasant and dangerous accuracy with what actually occurs

PUT, 'put it by', thrust it aside; 'put on', assume (I ii 298); show (I iii 60); betray (by revealing) (II i 225); 'put up', sheathed (I iii 19)

QUALITY, nature, character, natural disposition; 'from quality and kind', act contrary to their proper natures; 'monstrous quality', abnormal state; 'true quality', its proper, rightful, stable and resolute quality
QUARREL, (legal) accusation, charge
QUARTERED, cut into pieces
QUESTION (n.), crux, point at issue (II i 13); considerations that made the death necessary (III ii 36); 'call in question', deliberate upon
QUICK, I ii 29, (i) swift (in running); (ii) lively, vivacious; 'quick mettle', of a lively disposition (Cassius takes this to mean 'of steady courage', I ii 296)

RABBLEMENT, mob, crowd of common people
RAISE, rouse (IV iii 245)
RANGE, (of a falcon), soar, rove, in search of prey
RANK (adj.), swollen with disease (hence needing to be cured by blood-letting); (n.), position, dignity, order
RASCAL COUNTERS, worthless coins (see COUNTERS)
RASH, inflammable, explosive (IV iii 39); 'rash humour', irascible temperament
RATED, scolded, rebuked
RAVENS, CROWS, AND KITES, i.e. birds which were considered to be of ill omen
REASON (n.), i.e. my reason (II ii 104); (v.), 'Let's reason . . . befall', (proverbial), let us consider what is to be done if the worst happens
REBEL BLOOD, an unreliable disposition, uncontrollable passions
RECEIVEST THY FULL PETITION, you will be granted all you ask
RE-COVER, (i) patch; (ii) restore to health; (pun)
REEK, give off an unwholesome vapour, steam
REGARD (n.), 'good regard', sound, valid considerations; 'full of regard', worthy of respect; (v.), observe (V iii 21); respect, honour (V iii 88)
RELICS, objects used as a memorial of a martyr or saint (here, perhaps, some such thing as a handkerchief dipped in blood, see III ii 133)
REMORSE, compassion, pity

RENDER'D, uttered in return, retorted
REPAIR, make your way to
REPEAL (n.), recall from banishment
REPEALING, recalling from banishment
REPLICATION, reverberation, echo
REPUTE HIMSELF, consider himself to be
RESOLV'D, have his doubts and perplexities set at rest by being informed (III i 132); learnt for certain (III ii 179); informed (IV ii 14)
RESORT, 'had resort to', visited
RESPECT (n.), 'of the best respect', of the highest esteem, reputation; 'have respect to', consider, bear in mind; 'in respect of', in comparison with; 'of good respect', of good reputation; (v.), 'respect not', pay no attention to, ignore
REST STILL, remain always
RESTING, unchanging, static
RETENTIVE, 'be retentive to the strength of spirit', confine and imprison a resolute mind
RHEUMY, which causes catarrh ('rheum') (as the air has not yet been 'purged' by the sun of excessive moisture, which was believed to cause rheum)
RIGHT, 'right form of war', proper battle order
RIGHT ON, plainly, without art
RIV'D, split, broken
ROME INDEED, pun on 'room' and 'Rome', both apparently pronounced in Elizabethan English in the same way; 'Rome of safety', a similar pun
ROOM, 'way and room', freedom of action, of scope
ROTE, 'by rote', mechanically, by heart, without understanding
ROUND, rung (of a ladder) (II i 24)
ROUT, crowd of common people
ROYAL, noble, munificent
RUBBISH, refuse material, litter (such as results from the decay or repair of buildings, and is (here) suitable for tinder)
RUDDY DROPS, i.e. blood (see VISIT)
RUDE, barbarous, ignorant
RUDENESS, rough, blunt, manner
RUFFLE UP, stir up to indignation
RUL'D, had his way (i.e. about the treatment of Antony after Caesar's death), V i 47
RUMOUR, sound, murmur

SAD, serious, grave
SATISFIED, have his doubts (about allowing the return of Ligarius' brother from exile) removed, III i 48; have our doubts removed (III ii 1); given a full explanation (IV ii 10)

99

SAUCY, insolent, insulting; 'saucy with', insolent to
SAVING OF, when I spared
SCANDAL, defame, slander
SCAP'D, escaped
SCARF, a ceremonial strip of cloth used to adorn an image
SCHEDULE, paper, document
SCOPE, freedom to exist, free rein
SEARCH, probe, penetrate
SEAT HIM SURE, seat himself securely
SECOND (v.), support
SECOND FIGHT, (historically, the second battle took place twenty days later)
SECRET ROMANS . . . WORD, than that of the fact that we are Romans who have pledged ourselves, and will hold our tongues
SECURITY GIVES WAY TO, over-confidence in your security, lack of caution, leaves an opportunity for
SENATORS, members of the Roman Senate, the administrative body, composed largely of aristocratic 'patricians', which was charged with the highest deliberative functions in the Roman state
SENNET, series of trumpet-notes
SENSELESS, without feelings
SENSES, reason, understanding
SENSIBLE OF, feeling
SERVANTS, i.e. passions, emotions
SERV'D, attended to, dealt with (III i 8)
SET, stake (in gambling) (V i 74); 'Set honour in one eye . . . fear death' (I ii 86–89), 'if I am presented with the prospect of death with honour, I shall look on both with indifference, for, as I hope the gods may cause me to prosper, I assert that I value an honourable reputation more than I fear death', or 'if I am presented with the prospect of death with honour, I shall look on both with indifference, believing that the gods shall make me fortunate in direct proportion to the extent to which I value honour more highly than death'; 'set on', proceed, move onward; 'set on your foot', set off, begin walking
SEVERAL, separate, individual
SEVERALLY, separately
SHADOW, reflection, image
SHALLOWS, water too shallow to navigate with safety
SHAM'ST THOU, are you ashamed
SHOW, manifestation (I ii 34, I ii 47)
SHREWD CONTRIVER, malicious, mischievous plotter

SHREWDLY, unpleasantly, dangerously, accurately
SICK, 'sick offence', harmful sickness; 'make sick', i.e. kill
SIDE, side of (III ii 250); 'the other side', i.e. the other wing, of which Cassius is in command (V ii 2)
SIGN, 'sign of your profession', distinguishing marks, characteristics, of your trade (in this case, leather apron); 'bloody sign of battle', i.e. a red flag (the Roman signal for battle); 'sign of battle', signal to commence battle (V i 23)
SIGN'D IN, marked by, bearing the bloody tokens of
SINK IN THE TRIAL, fail when put to the test
SIRRAH, term of address expressing contempt, reprimand, or assumption of authority on the part of the speaker
SLAUGHTER, 'Till another Caesar . . . by traitors' hands', till yet another Caesar (i.e. Octavius) shall have been slain by the swords of traitors
SLIGHT, insignificant, worthless; 'slight unmeritable', insignificant and unworthy of consideration
SLIGHTED OFF, slightingly disregarded
SLIP, 'let slip', unleash
SLIPPERY GROUND, (i) an equivocal, uncertain, position (for he was an intimate friend of Caesar); (ii) (perhaps) an allusion to Caesar's blood, covering the floor beneath them
SMATCH, smack, taste
SO, 'so please him', if it should please him to, if he would be so good as to
SOBER FORM, grave and restrained demeanour
SOFT, stop, wait
SOFTLY, slowly (V i 16)
SOIL, blemish, stain (I ii 42)
SOLES, (i) undersides of shoes, (ii) souls; (pun)
SON OF CAESAR, perhaps an allusion to Caesar's words 'And thou, my son?' to Brutus as he was stabbed, as reported by the Roman writer Suetonius
SOOTH, in truth
SOOTHSAYER, one who claims professionally to be able to foretell the future
SOPHIST, in ancient Greece, one who gave instruction in intellectual and ethical matters in return for payment
SORT, class (I i 58); way, manner (I ii 205); 'in sort', after a fashion (allusion to the legal

terminology of documents connected with land-tenure)

SOUND, utter (I ii 145); 'sound him', find out his feeling about this; 'sounded more', be uttered more, i.e. resound more in fame

SPACE, 'mighty space of our large honours', the powerful and honourable offices which lie in our power to confer

SPANIEL, obsequious, flattering (metaphor taken from the fawning of a dog)

SPARE, lean, abstemious

SPEED, favour me, make me prosper (I ii 88); grant you speed and success (II iv 40)

SPIRIT OF CAESAR, i.e. what Caesar represents (with pun on 'spirit' = 'soul', II i 168)

SPIRITS, tendencies (I iii 69)

SPLEEN, organ thought to be the seat of sudden passions, i.e. 'venom of your spleen' = poison of your bad, irritable, temper

SPOIL, (in hunting) capture of the quarry and its distribution to the hounds, i.e. (here) 'slaughter' (III i 207); 'spoils', plunder, acts of pillage

SPOT, i.e. 'prick', mark (IV i 6)

SPUR, 'on the spur', at a gallop (spurring hard)

SPURN, kick

STABB'D THEIR MOTHERS, (i) killed their mothers with a knife; (ii) (perhaps) made love to their mothers; (innuendo)

STAKE, 'at the stake', tied to the stake (like a bear in bear-baiting, to prevent its escape)

STALE . . . PROTESTER, make stale, cheapen, the value of my love by professing it with oaths that are commonplace, habitual, or fit only for the tavern (see ORDINARY) to every new acquaintance who professed affection for me

STAND (n.), position at which I shall stand (II iv 24); (v.), halt (IV ii 1); may they be (V i 93); 'stands as the Capitol', is situated where the Capitol is; 'standing', i.e. preparing to resist possible attack (III i 90); 'stand upon', attach importance to; 'stood', considered valid (III ii 119); 'stood on ceremonies', attached much importance to omens

STARE, stand wide-eyed in astonishment (III i 98); glare in anger (IV iii 40); stand upright (IV iii 278)

STARS, allusion to the belief in astrology, i.e. that the life of a man would be predetermined by the configuration of the heavenly bodies at the instant of his birth (I ii 140)

START (n.), 'get the start of', (in running)

outstrip and thus win the prize; (v.), startle, raise

STATE, state of affairs (I iii 71, III i 137); kingdom, realm (II i 67); 'keep his state', maintain his court

STATILIUS, (in Plutarch, Statilius had volunteered to make his way to the camp through the enemy troops, and to hold up a torch to indicate if all was well there)

STATUA, statue

STAY, often, 'wait'; keep, retain (II ii 75); prevent (IV iii 126); 'stay the providence', await and endure the fate ordained us by

STEAD, place

STEEL (v.), make firm, resolute

STEMMING, breasting, making headway against

STILL, (adj.), 'Caesar now be still', allusion to the belief that a ghost, once avenged, can rest in peace; (adv.), always

STOMACH, appetite, i.e. inclination

STORE, a supply (IV i 30)

STRAIGHT, straightaway, immediately

STRAIN, tune (IV iii 255); lineage, stock (V i 59)

STRANGE, estranged, hostile (I ii 35)

STRANGE-DISPOSED, extraordinary, abnormal

STREAM, 'lowest stream', water level even at the lowest ebb

STRETCH'D, made to go as far as possible (IV i 44)

STRUCK . . . FIRE, metaphor from the striking of flint and steel to produce a spark with which to light a fire

STRUCKEN, stricken (used of a deer wounded in the chase)

STUBBORN, tightly controlled, unforthcoming, unyielding

SUBURBS, 'Dwell I but in the suburbs . . . pleasure?', Is my role only to be that of the gratification of your physical lust? (allusion to the fact that the London brothels were situated in the 'suburb' of Southwark)

SUCCESS, the result (whether good or bad); 'my success', the result of my mission

SUDDEN, quick, speedy (III i 19)

SUFFERANCE, I iii 84, see YOKE AND SUFFERANCE; distress and suffering (II i 115)

SUFFERING, submissive, inured to suffering

SUIT, petition (II iv 26, III i 6)

SUITOR, like one who petitions (II iii 9); petitioner (III i 228, II iv 34)

SUP, drink, take supper

SURE, securely, safely (I ii 320)

SWAY, 'all the sway of earth', the whole weight, momentum (or 'government', 'dominion') of the earth

SWAY'D, ruled him (II i 20); distracted, diverted (III i 220)

SWEAR PRIESTS . . . , let priests . . . rely on oaths

SWORD-HILTS, sword-hilt

SWORE THEE, SAVING OF, made you swear when I spared

TA'EN, captured

TAG-RAG PEOPLE, common rabble

TAKE, take advantage of, set sail upon (IV iii 217, IV iii 221); 'ta'en', captured; 'take note of', set eyes on (V iii 50); 'take thought', give way to melancholy (induced by sorrow at the death of Caesar)

TAPER, candle

TARDY FORM, pretence of slow-wittedness

TARQUIN, Tarquinius Collatinus, one of the Tarquins, the legendary early dynasty of Roman kings (see BRUTUS)

TARRYING, 'there is no tarrying here', here is not a fit place to delay, loiter

TASTE, 'in some taste', in some degree

TEETH, 'show'd your teeth', grinned, smiled insincerely

TEMPER, temperament, constitution; 'Of brother's temper', full of a brotherly regard (for you)

TEMPT, make trial of, defy (I iii 53); 'defy' and 'risk' (II i 266); provoke (IV iii 36)

TENDING ON, concerning, relating to

TENDING TO, relating to, bearing on

TENOUR, purport

TESTY, 'Under your testy humour', in accordance with your irritable and irascible temper

THASOS, island near Philippi, off the coast of Thrace

THAT, the inclination that (see DISPOS'D) (I ii 309)

THEREFORE, I ii 66, (i) with respect to that; (ii) i.e. Cassius brushes aside Brutus' objection of I ii 63–5; for that reason (III i 219)

THEREIN, i.e. in the capacity to commit suicide (I iii 91)

THESE AND THESE EXTREMITIES, such and such extremes (of severity or tyranny)

THEWS, sinews

THICK, dim (V iii 21)

THING, 'Art thou any thing?', do you have a real existence independent of my imagination (or are you merely an illusion generated by my own mind)?; 'thing as I myself', i.e. of another (Caesar) who is a mere man just like me

THINK HIM AS, consider him to be like

THIS, 'by this', by this time (I iii 125)

THOROUGH, through

THOUGHT, 'even with a thought', as swift as thought

THREEFOLD WORLD DIVIDED, once the world has been split into three (allusion to either (i) the Roman division of the world into Europe, Africa, and Asia; or (ii) the conditions upon which the Triumvirate, the joint reign of Octavius, Antony, and Lepidus over the Roman world, was established in the autumn of 43 B C, i.e. that Octavius was to control Africa, Sardinia and Sicily, Antony Gaul, and Lepidus Spain)

THUNDERSTONE, thunderbolt, bolt of lightning

TIDE OF TIMES, the course of history

TIME, 'knows his time', knows the right time for it

TINCTURES, (i) stains; (ii) (in heraldry) colours; (iii) (in alchemy) a supposed spiritual principle or immaterial substance whose character or quality might be infused into material things, which were then said to be 'tinctured'

TO, fit to (I iii 40); as much applicable to (II ii 29); 'well to friend', safely as a good friend; 'all that he can do is to himself', the only harm he can do is to himself, that is

TOILS, nets, snares

TO-NIGHT, last night

TOUCH, concern (III i 8); play upon (IV iii 255); 'touches Caesar nearer', more particularly concerns Caesar himself

TOUCHING (adj.), grievous

TOWARD, that concerns (I ii 85)

TRADE, craft

TRAIN, group of attendants, retinue

TRASH, twigs, splinters, cuttings from a hedge (i.e. rubbish suitable for tinder) (I iii 108); money (IV iii 26, IV iii 74)

TRIBUNES, officers appointed to protect the interest and rights of the common people of Rome from the 'patricians' (the governing aristocracy, the senators)

TRIBUTARIES, captives who will pay tribute

TRICKS, artifices

TRIUMPH, triumphal procession to celebrate a

military victory; 'in triumph', in a triumphal procession

TRIUMVIRS, members of the 'Second Triumvirate', the coalition of 43 B C of Antony, Octavius and Lepidus, as supreme governors of the Roman world

TROPHIES, ornaments symbolising a triumph in honour of Caesar

TROUBLE, 'turn the trouble of . . . myself', 'I direct the look of anxiety on my face towards myself (as it is with myself and not with others that I am angry)', or 'I direct the look of anxiety (which would normally be expressed upon my face when feeling such an emotion) inwards against myself (and hence appear aloof)'

TRUE, honest (I ii 260); fitting, proper (III i 242)

TRUE-FIX'D, immovable

TRY, test (III i 293)

TURN, reflect (I ii 56); 'turn back', return alive; 'turn him going', send him packing

'TWEEN, between

UNBRACED, with doublet unfastened

UNDER, according to, in accordance with (IV iii 46); 'Under your pardon', if you will forgive me for contradicting you

UNDERGO, undertake

UNFIRM, unsteady, unstable

UNGENTLE, discourteous, disrespectful

UNGENTLY, disrespectfully, discourteously

UNICORNS . . . TREES, allusion to the legendary method of catching a unicorn. The hunter stood in front of a tree and induced his prey to charge until, at the last moment, he dodged behind the tree, into whose trunk the unicorn irremovably impaled its single horn

UNKINDEST, (i) most unnatural; (ii) most cruel

UNKINDLY, (i) unnaturally; (ii) cruelly

UNMERITABLE, unworthy of consideration

UNNUMB'RED, uncounted, innumerable

UNPURGED, unpurified (by the heat of the sun, of excessive moisture)

UNSHAK'D OF MOTION, undisturbed by movement

UNTROD STATE, unknown, unfamiliar, state of affairs

UP, i.e. in full swing, upon us (V i 68)

UPMOST, highest

UPON, as a result of (IV iii 150); 'upon a wish', exactly according to my desire

URGE, suggest (II i 155); press for an answer

(II i 243); present (III i 11); harry, provoke (IV iii 35)

USE (n.), 'beyond all use', outside all customary experience, totally abnormal; 'in use', common; (v.), are accustomed (I ii 258); treat (V v 76); 'did use', was accustomed; 'hath us'd', was his custom

UTTERANCE, skilful elocution and delivery

UTTERED, emitted, sent forth

UTTERMOST, latest time

VAUNTING, boasting

VEIL'D MY LOOK, bore upon my face a troubled (or distant, aloof) expression

VENTURES, merchandise risked in trade

VESTURE, clothing

VILE, base, evil; worthless (I iii 111); bad in effect (II i 265); mean in rank (III ii 32)

VILLAGER, i.e. not a citizen of Rome

VILLAINS, i.e. his own men (V iii 1)

VISIT, II i 290, allusion to the Elizabethan theory that the blood was manufactured by the liver, and flowed thence to the heart, where it was purified and distributed to the rest of the body; 'visit other places', i.e. be elsewhere

VOICE, vote, authority (III i 178); vote, opinion (IV i 16)

VOID, 'more void', more empty, less crowded

VOUCHSAFE, deign to accept

VULGAR, common people

WAFTURE, waving gestures

WANT, lack

WARN, challenge

WASPISH, irascible

WAS'T, it was

WASTED, 'march is wasted fifteen days', today is 15 March

WATCH (n.), night-watch, night-guardsmen

WATCH YOUR PLEASURE, remain awake and watch for anything that you may wish us to do for you

WATCHFUL CARES, anxieties which cause sleeplessness

WAY AND ROOM, freedom of action, scope

WEIGHING, considering, when one considers

WELL, 'as well', as easily, as fittingly (I ii 234); 'well to friend', safely as a good friend

WHAT, impatient exclamation (II i 5); 'What villain . . . justice', who that touched his body was so villainous to stab him for any motive other than a desire for justice?

WHELPED, given birth (to a cub)

WHEN, impatient exclamation, i.e. how long are you going to take? (II i 5)
WHE'R, whether
WHEREIN, with respect to which (i.e. his glory) (III ii 37)
WHEREOF, 'By means whereof', as a result of which (i.e. my mistake)
WHET, incite
WHILE, 'woe the while!', alas for these present times!
WHIT, tiny particle; 'no whit', not at all
WHIZZING, rushing along and hissing
WHO, whoever, he who (I iii 120)
WHOLE, sound, healthy (II i 327)
WILL, (arbitrary) desire, whim (II ii 71); 'with your will', as you wish; 'my will', what I myself desired to do (V iii 48)
WIND (v.), (in horsemanship), turn, wheel
WINDOWS, shutters
WISH, 'upon a wish', exactly according to my desires
WIT, intelligence; intellectual cleverness (III ii 221)
WITHAL, moreover, at the same time (II i 249); I am also, in addition (II i 292)
WOE THE WHILE!, alas for the present times!
WONDER, 'in wonder', into a state of astonishment
WONDERFUL, 'any thing more wonderful', 'anything else that was awesome', or 'anything that was more awesome (than the other paltry events which you describe)
WONT, accustomed
WORD, word of command, order (Lucilius is passing on Brutus's order to his subordinates) (IV ii 2); 'taken him at a word', behaved in accordance with his command; 'Speak the word along', pass the order along from one soldier to the next; 'words', eloquence, fluency (III ii 221)
WORK (v.), influence, persuade (I ii 163)
WORLD, the present state of affairs (I ii 306)
WORSE DAYS, i.e. greater and more unpleasant acts of tyranny, or days of punishment if the plot were to be discovered or fail
WORSHIPS, mock title of respect
WORTH, weight of authority with which to support my assertions, III ii 221
WORTHY, important (I ii 50); considerable (IV ii 8); 'worthy note', worthy of notice
WOULD, wishes to be (II i 12); wish to (V v 41)
WRATH, 'like wrath in death', as if the murder were motivated by personal animosity
WREATH OF VICTORY, allusion to the Roman custom of placing on the head of a victorious military leader a wreath, originally made out of the leaves of the palm
WRONG, harm (III i 243)
WROUGHT FROM, twisted away from

YEARNS, grieves, feels pity
YESTERNIGHT, last night
YIELDS HIM OURS, will surrender himself to our persuasion, join our cause
YOKE AND SUFFERANCE, submission to tyranny and willingness to accept it
YOKED WITH, associated (in your partnership with me) with